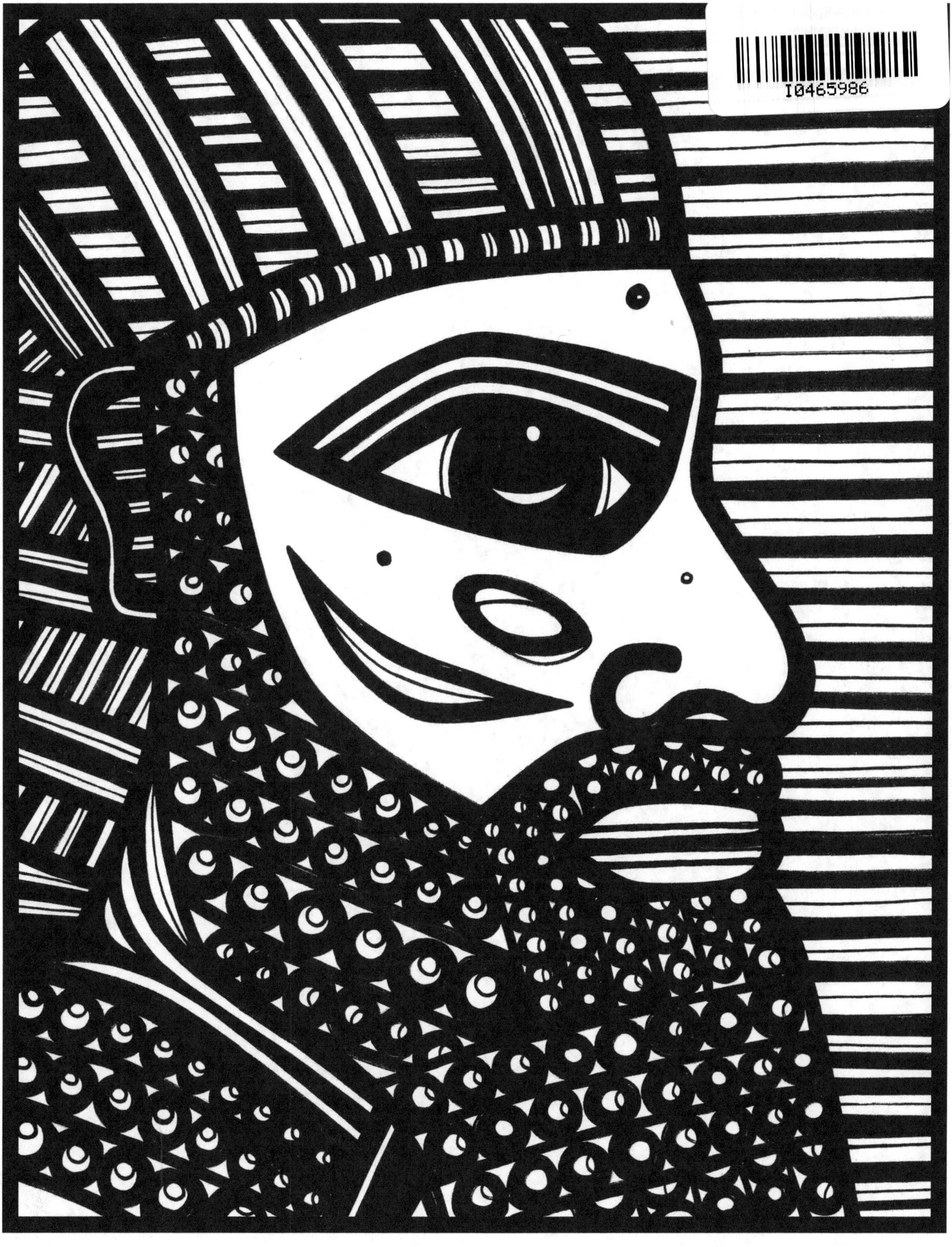

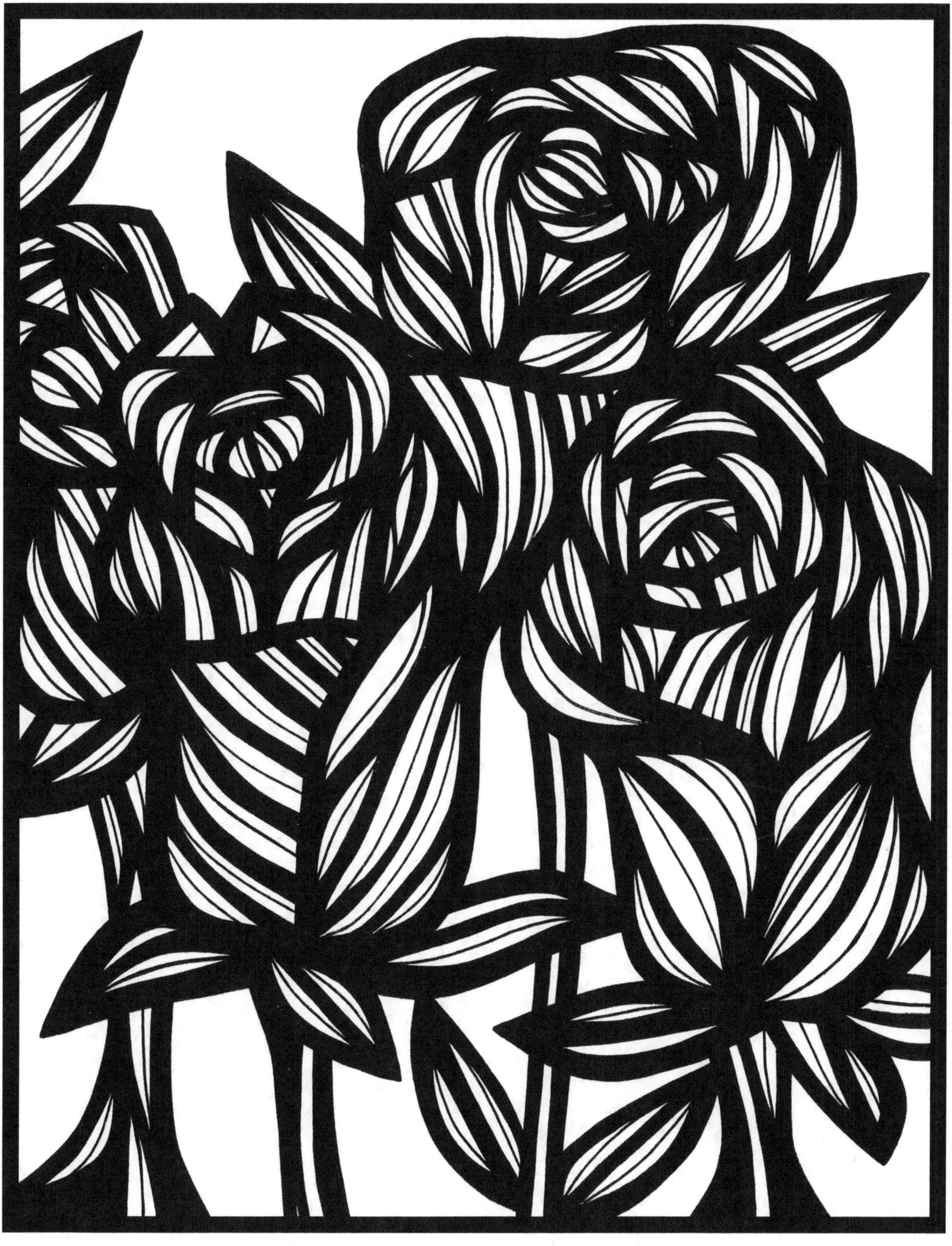

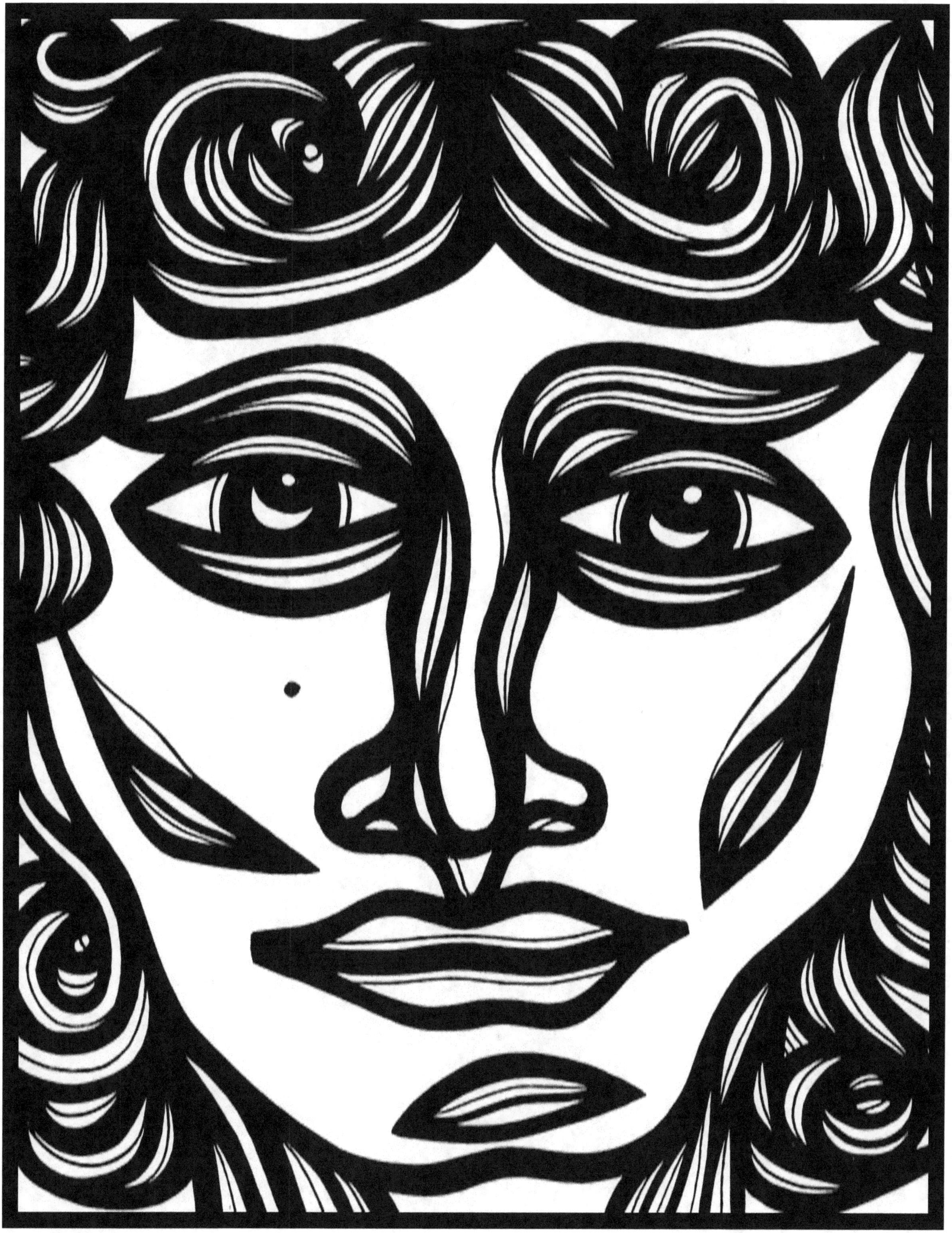

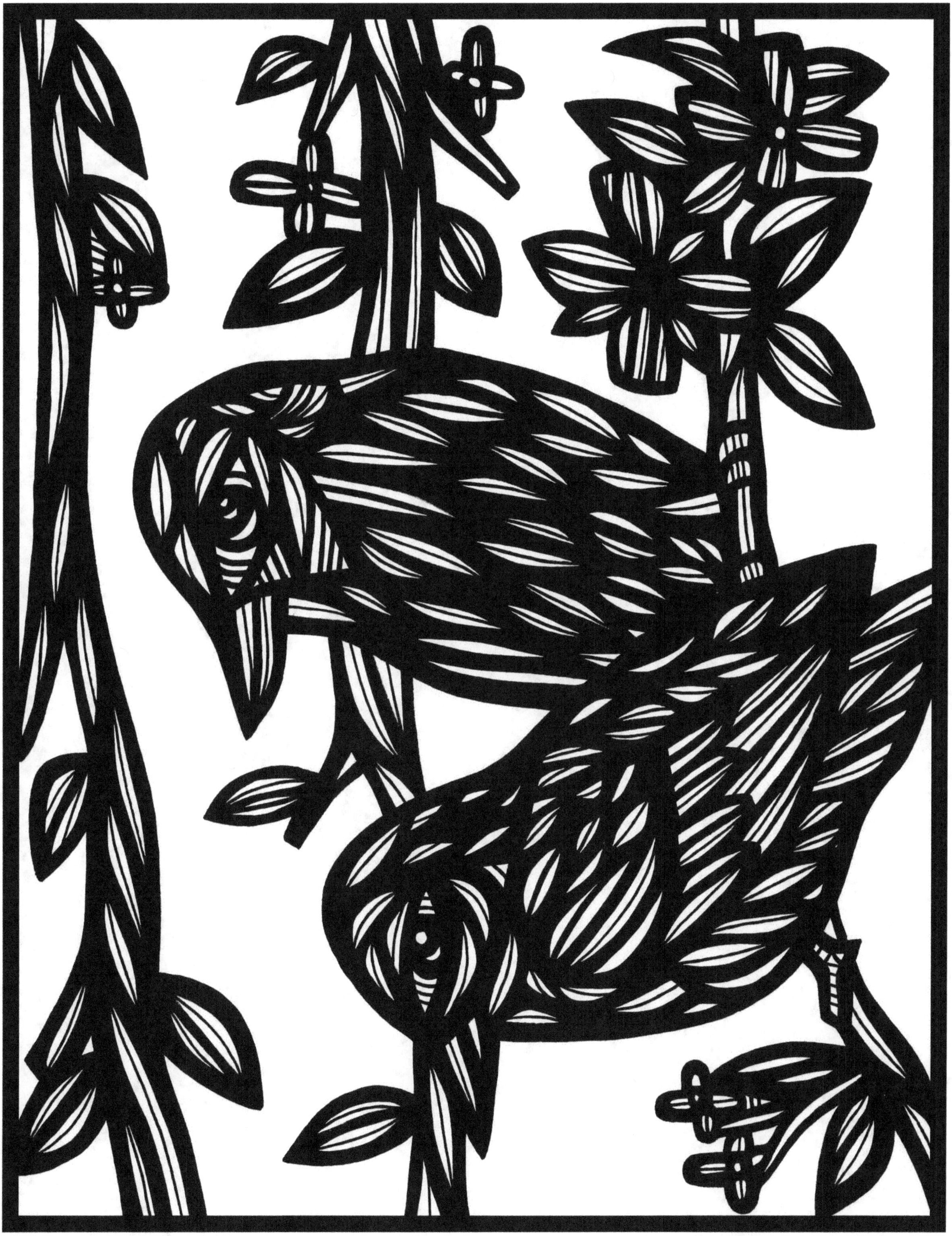

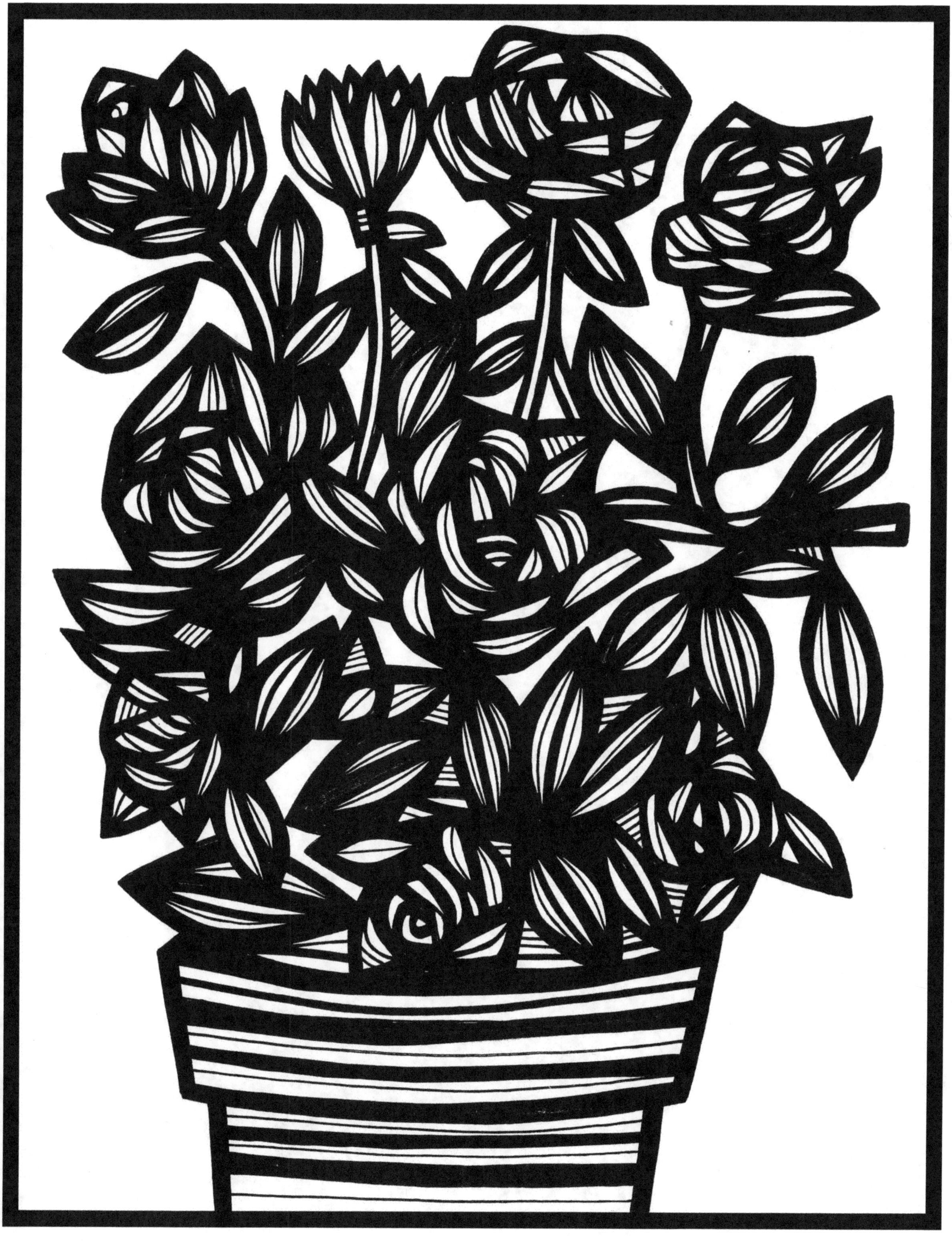

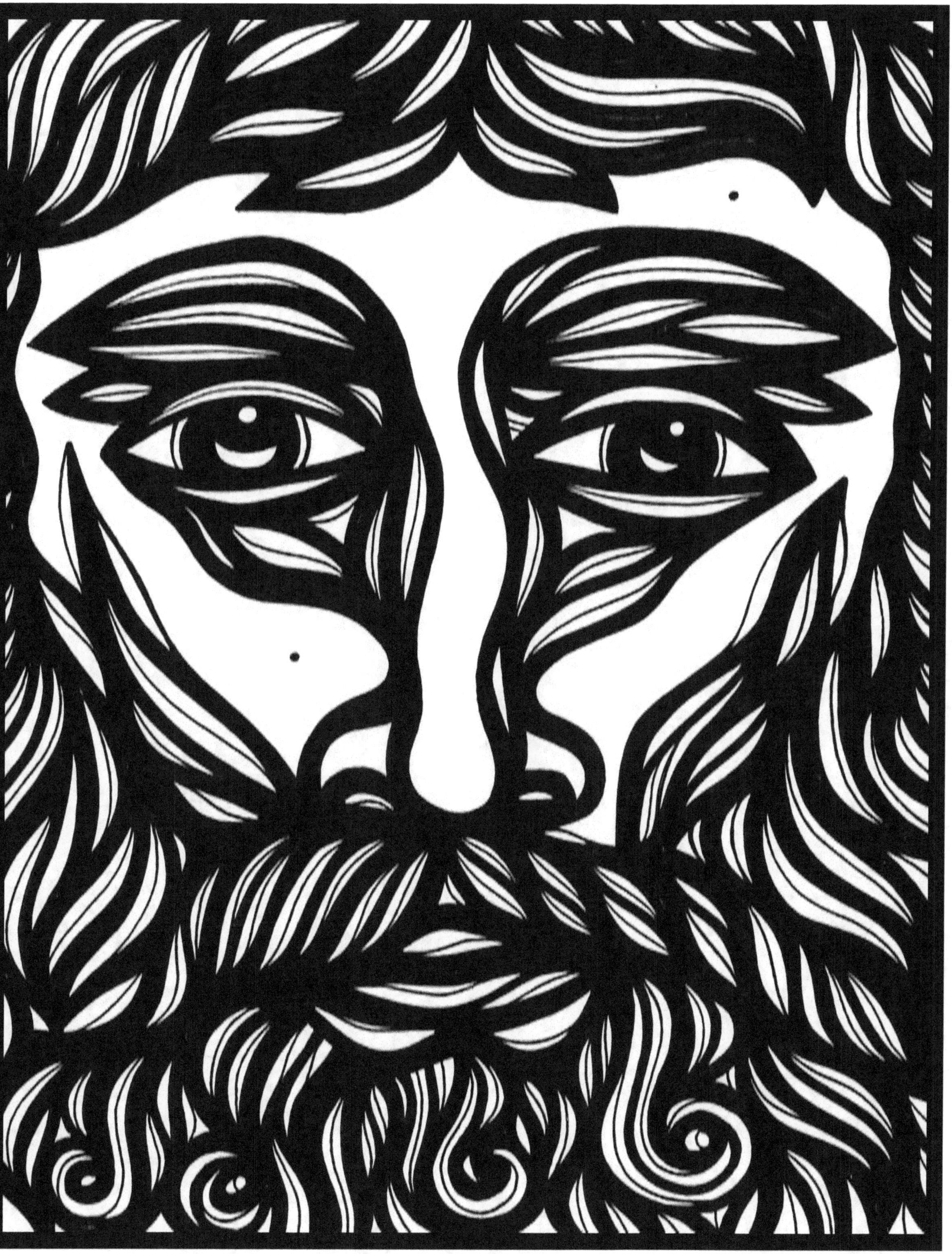

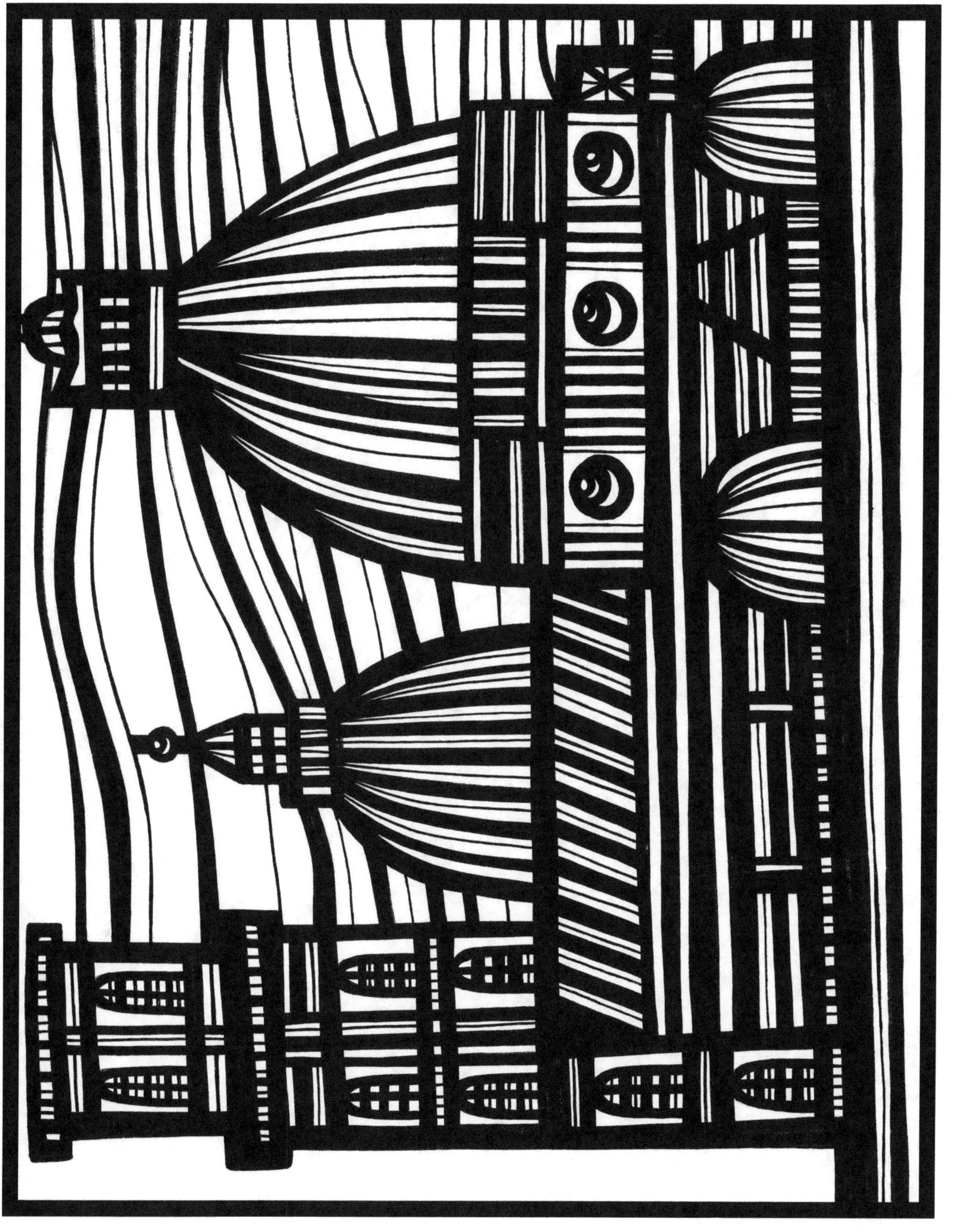

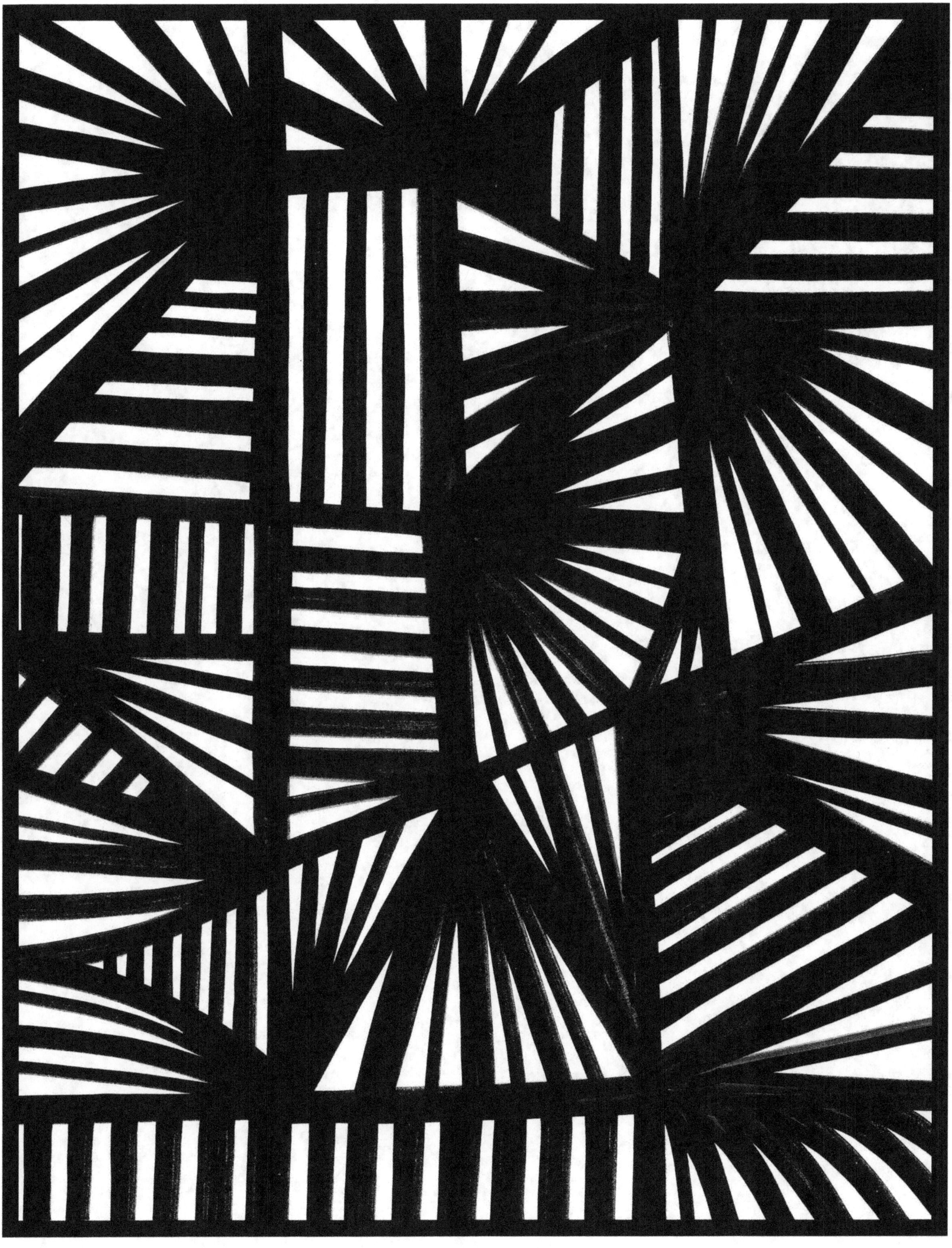

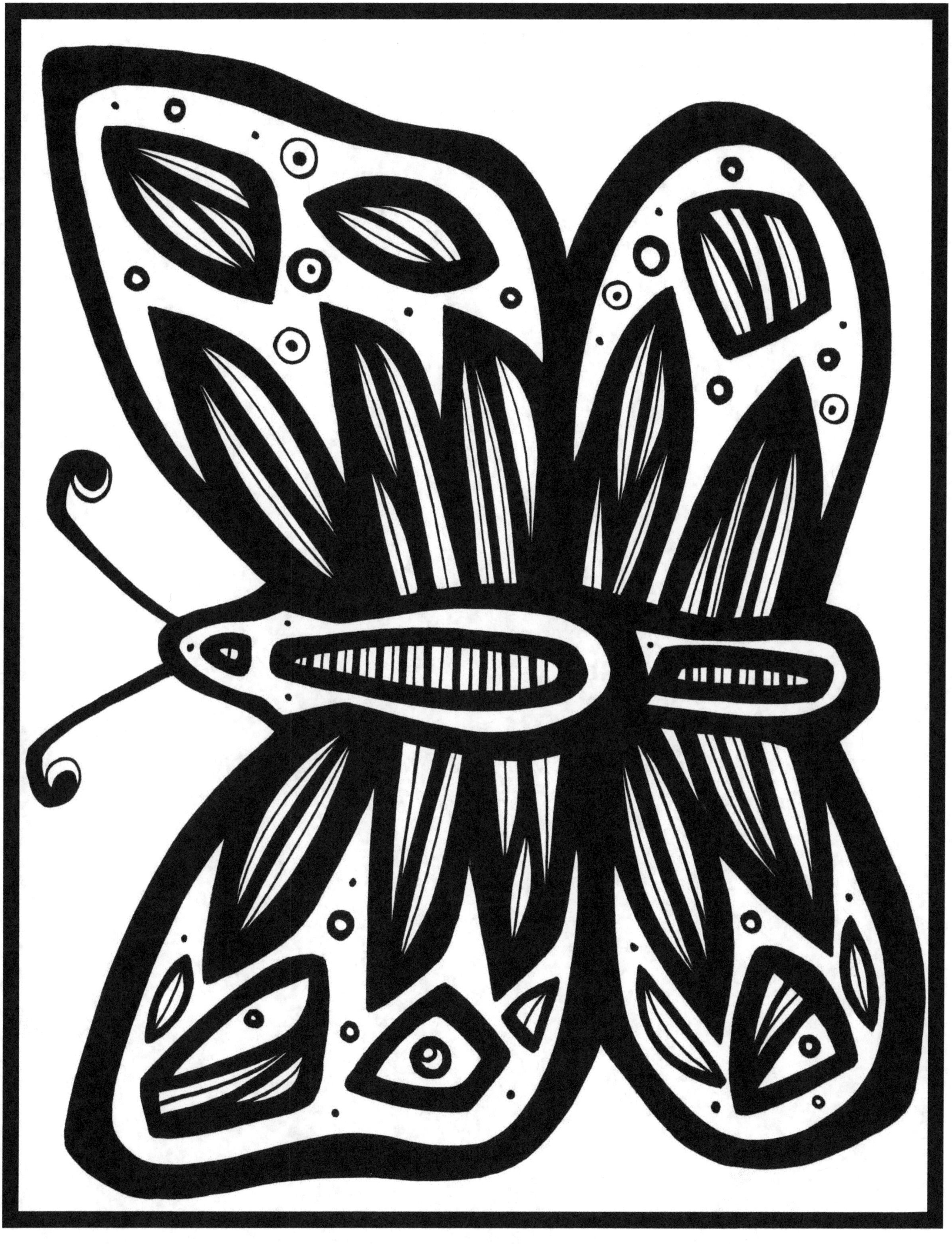

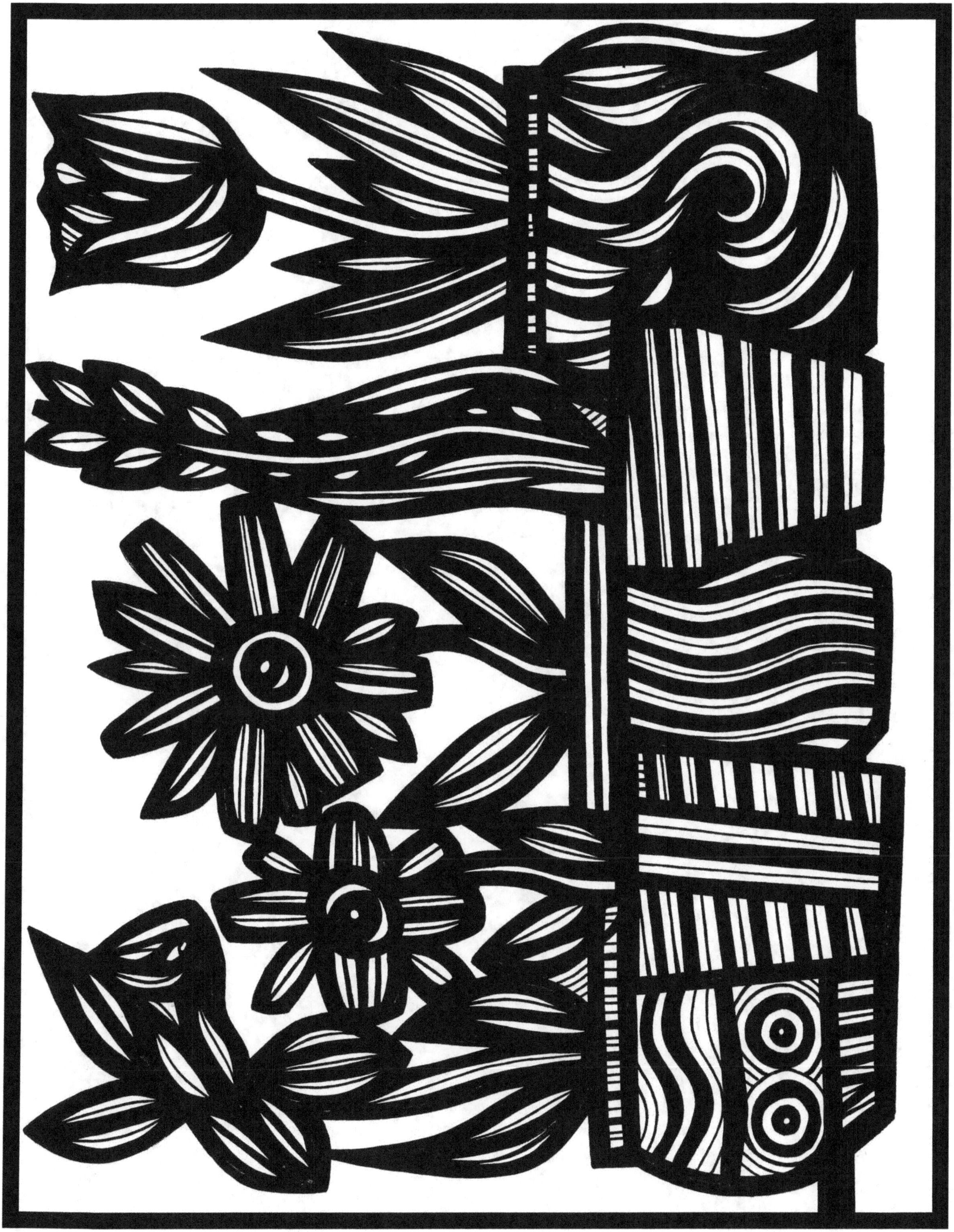

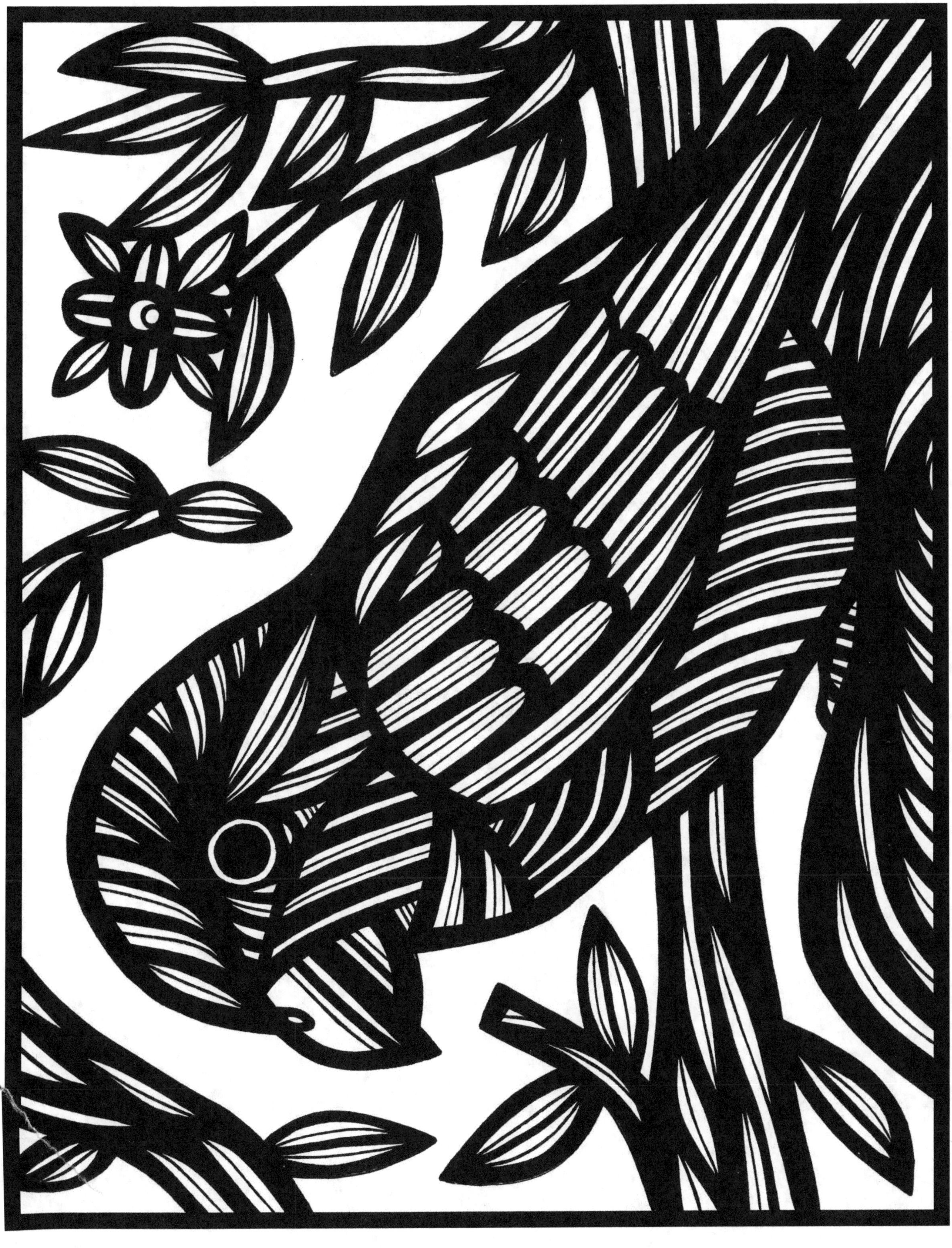

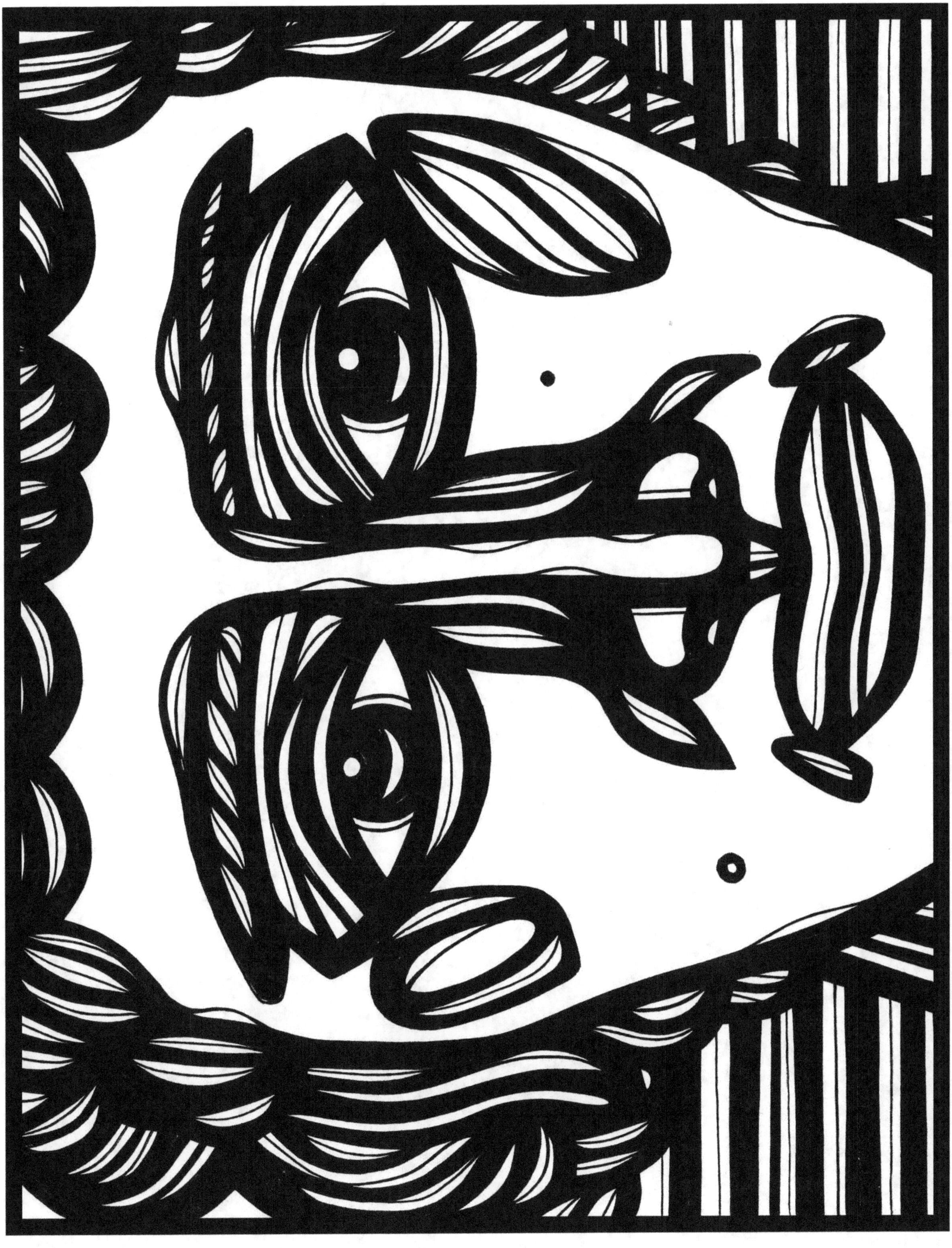

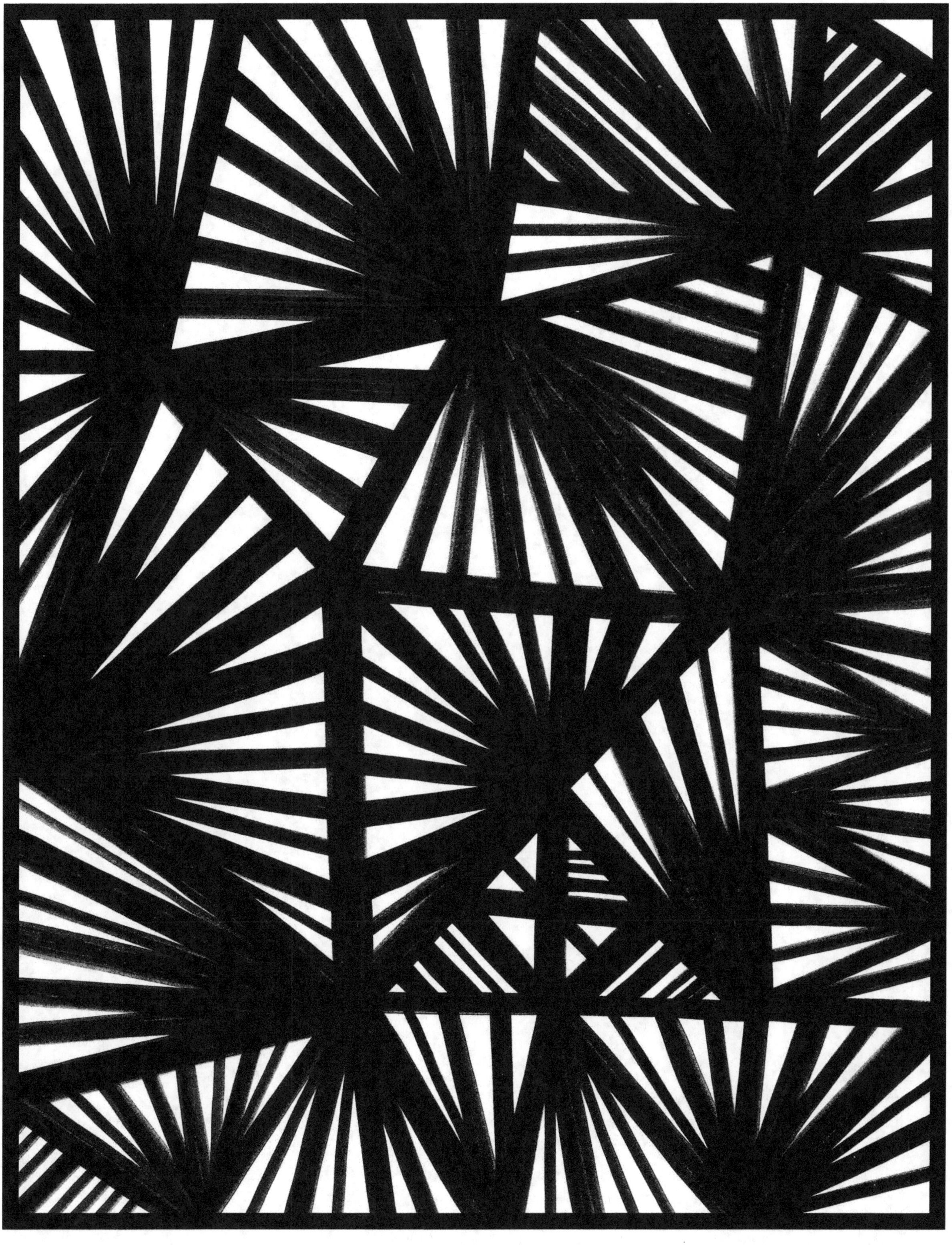

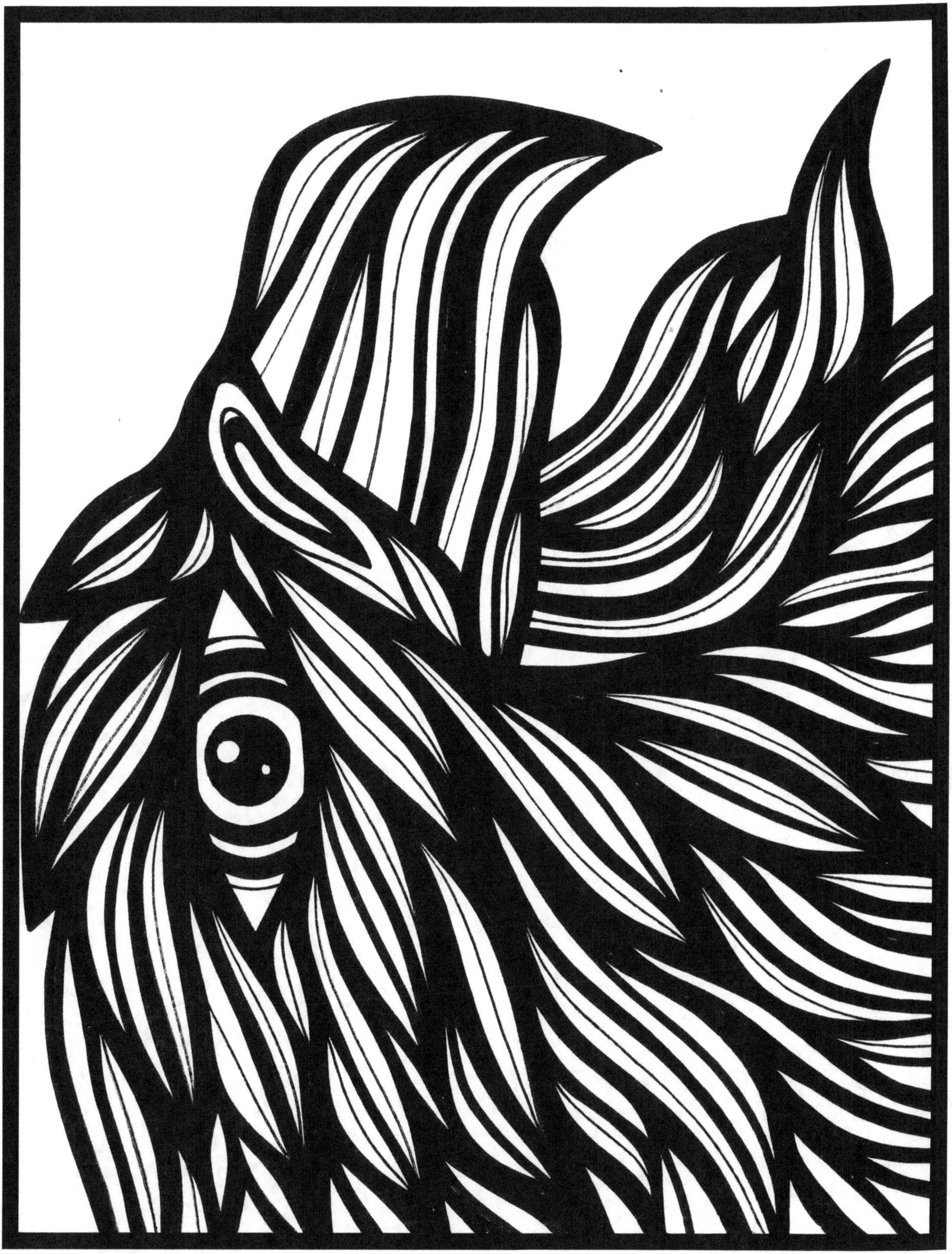

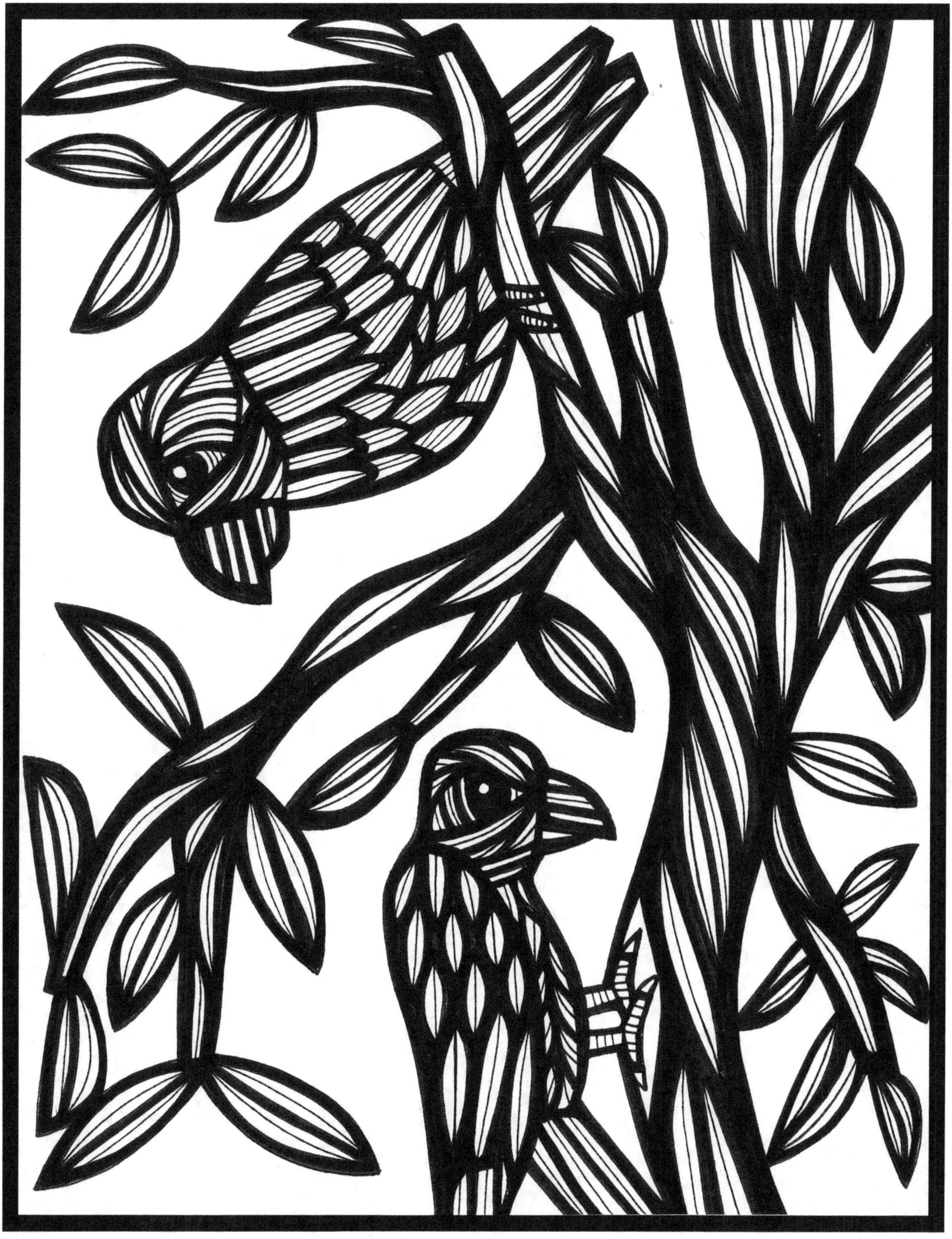

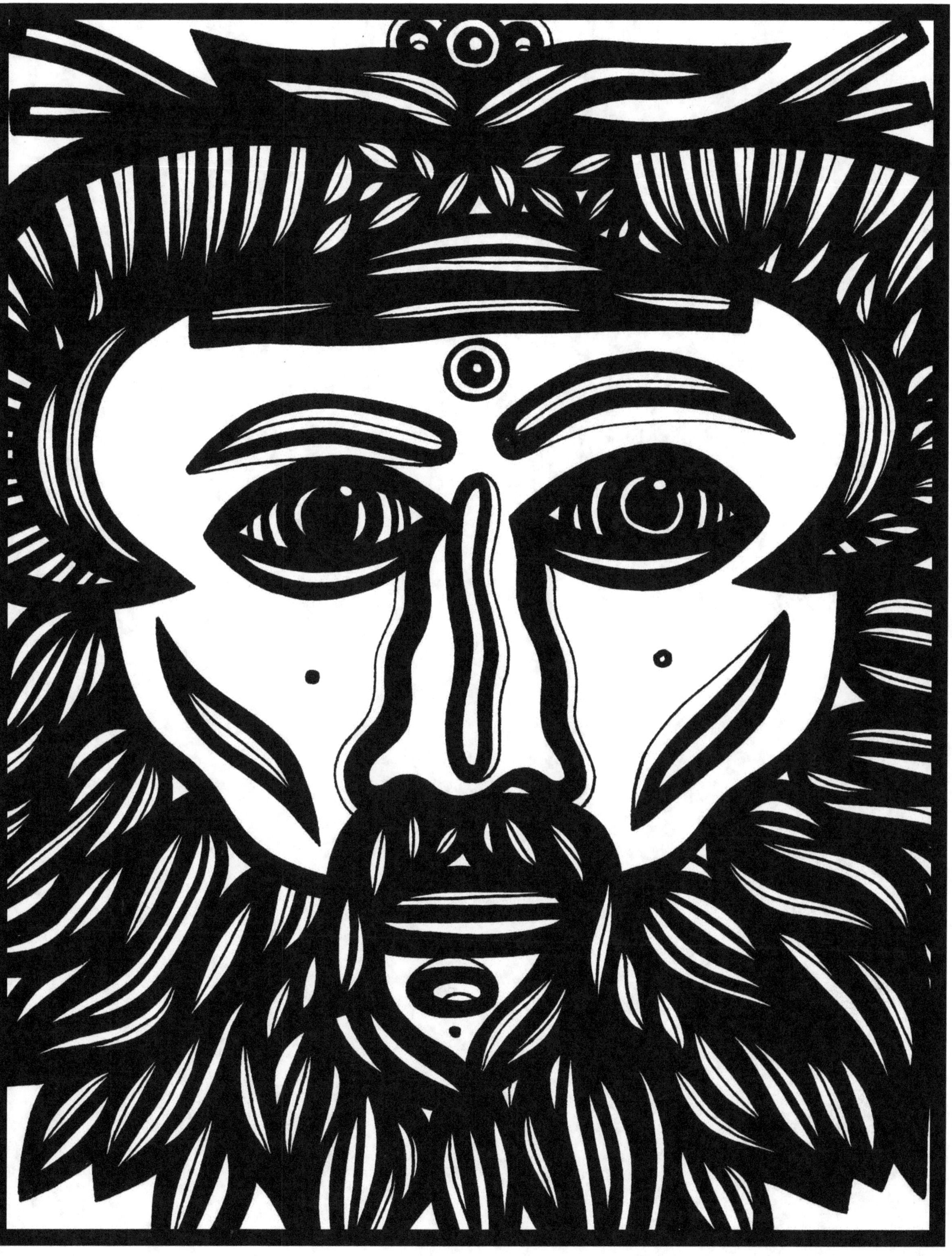

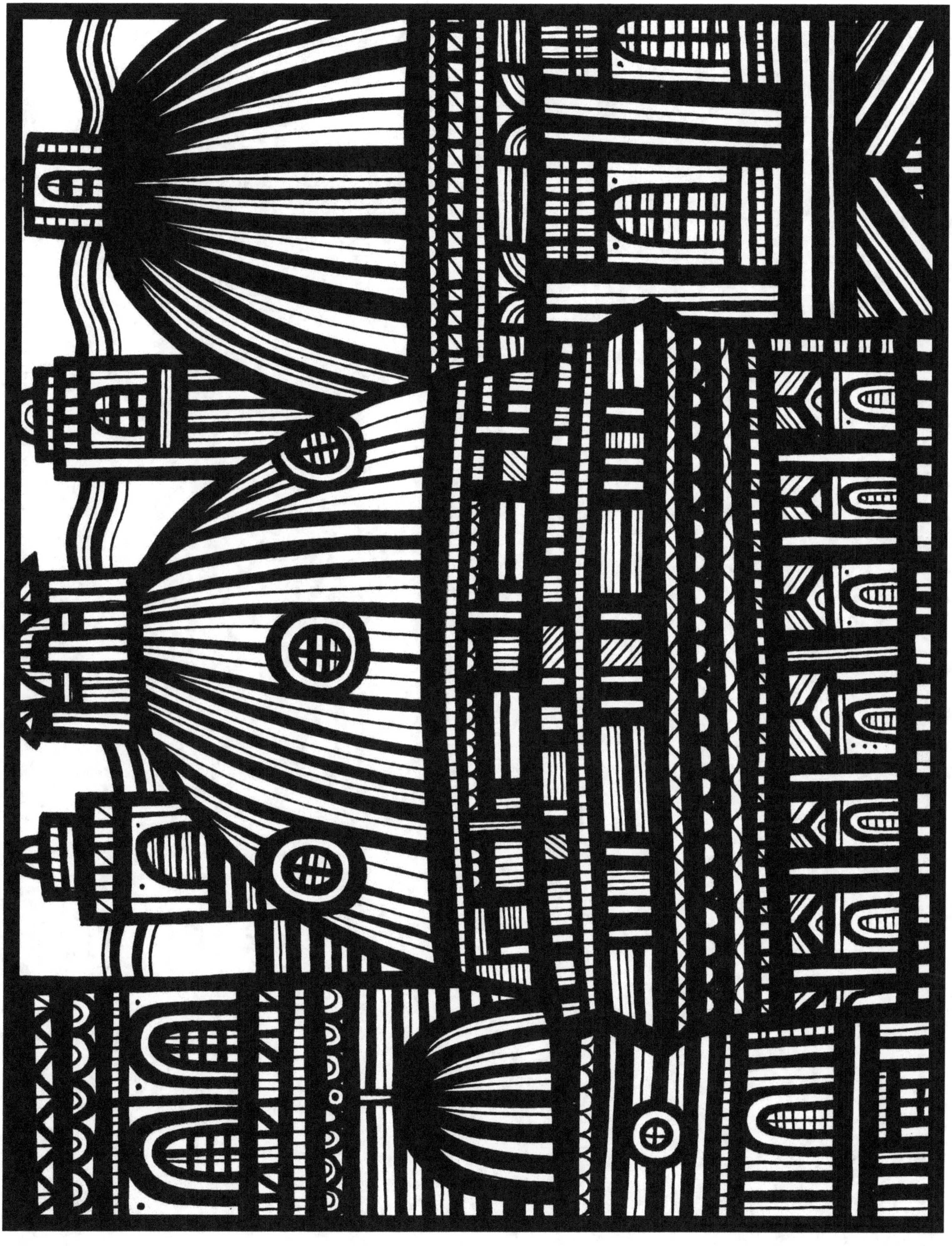

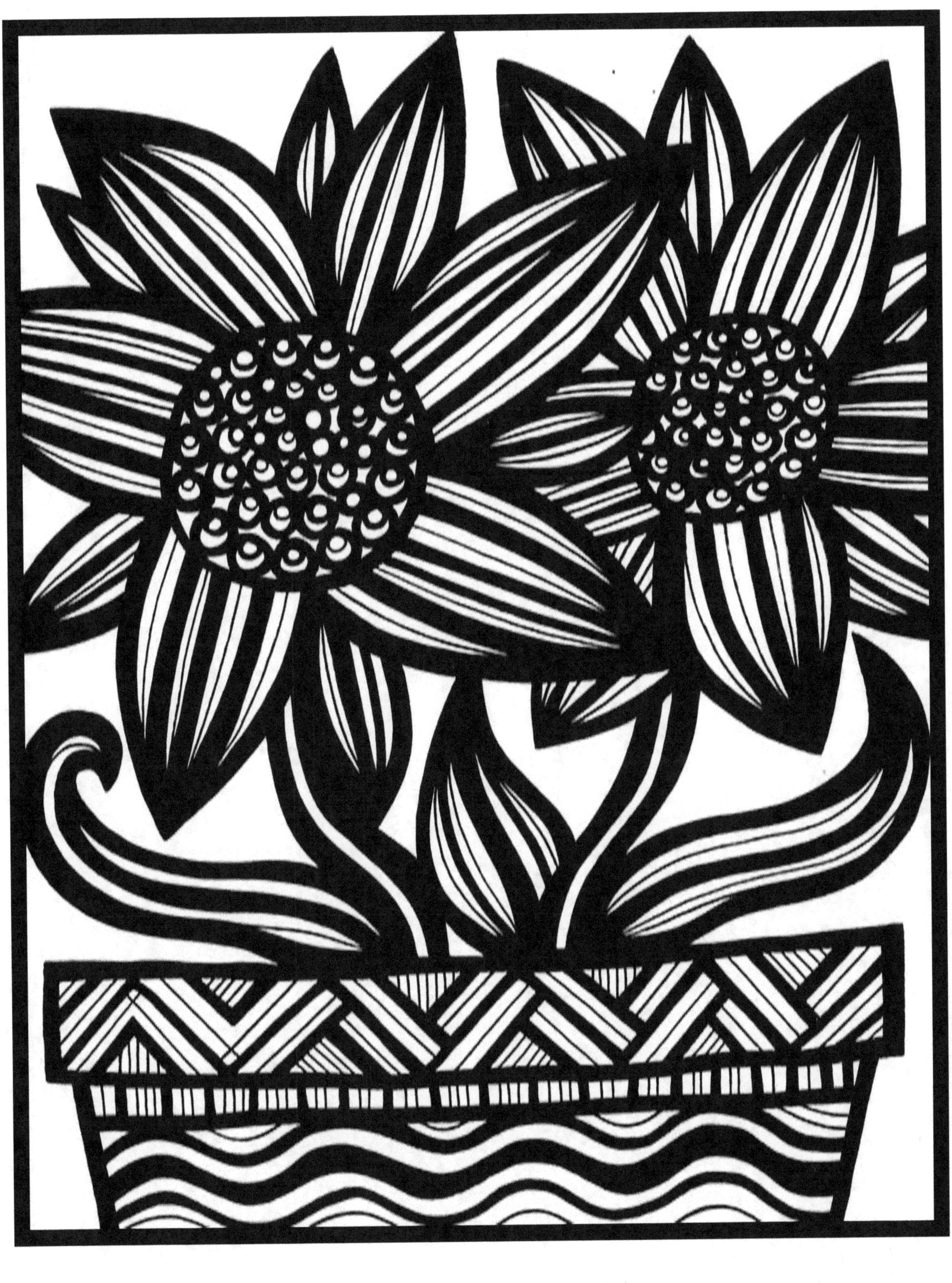

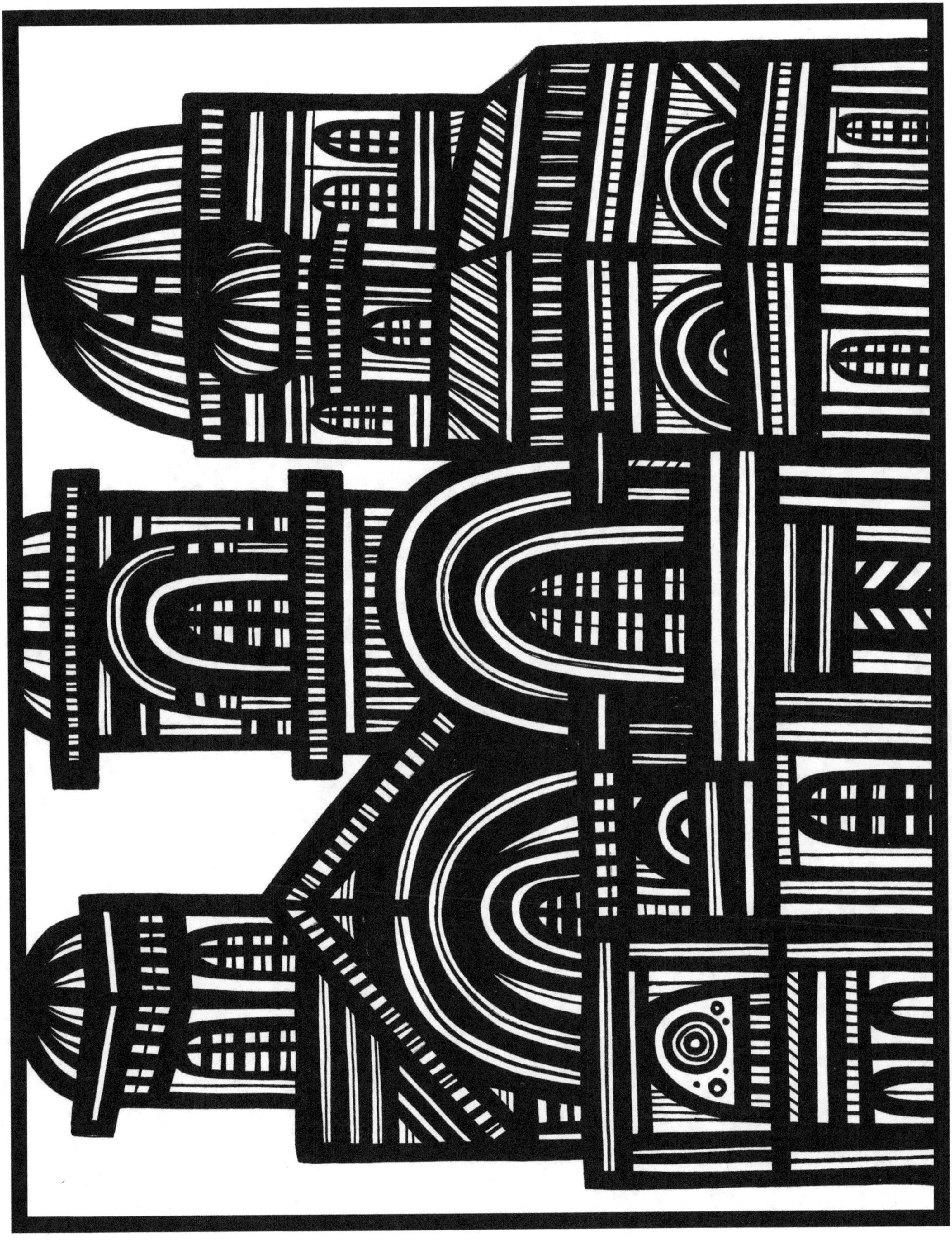

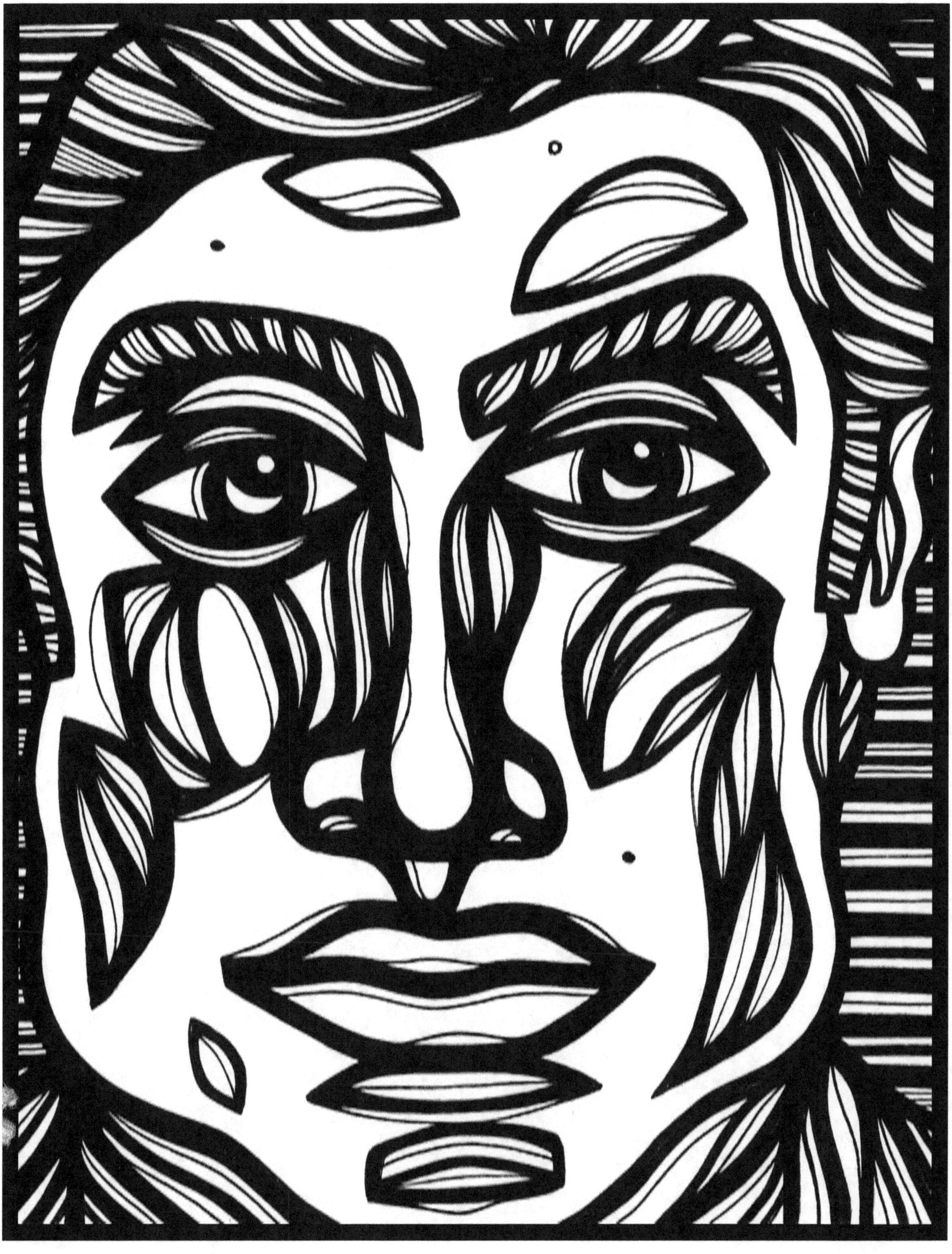

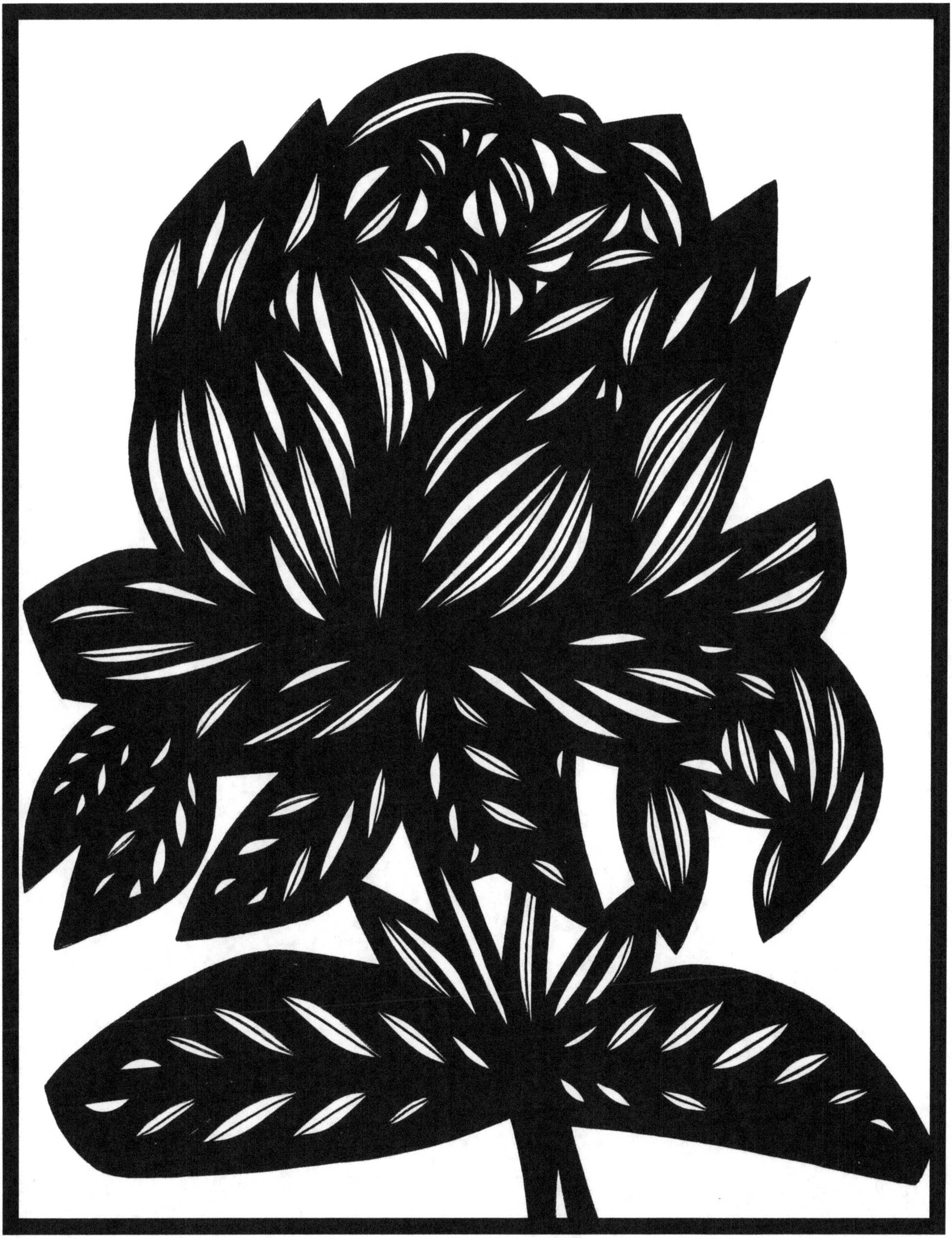

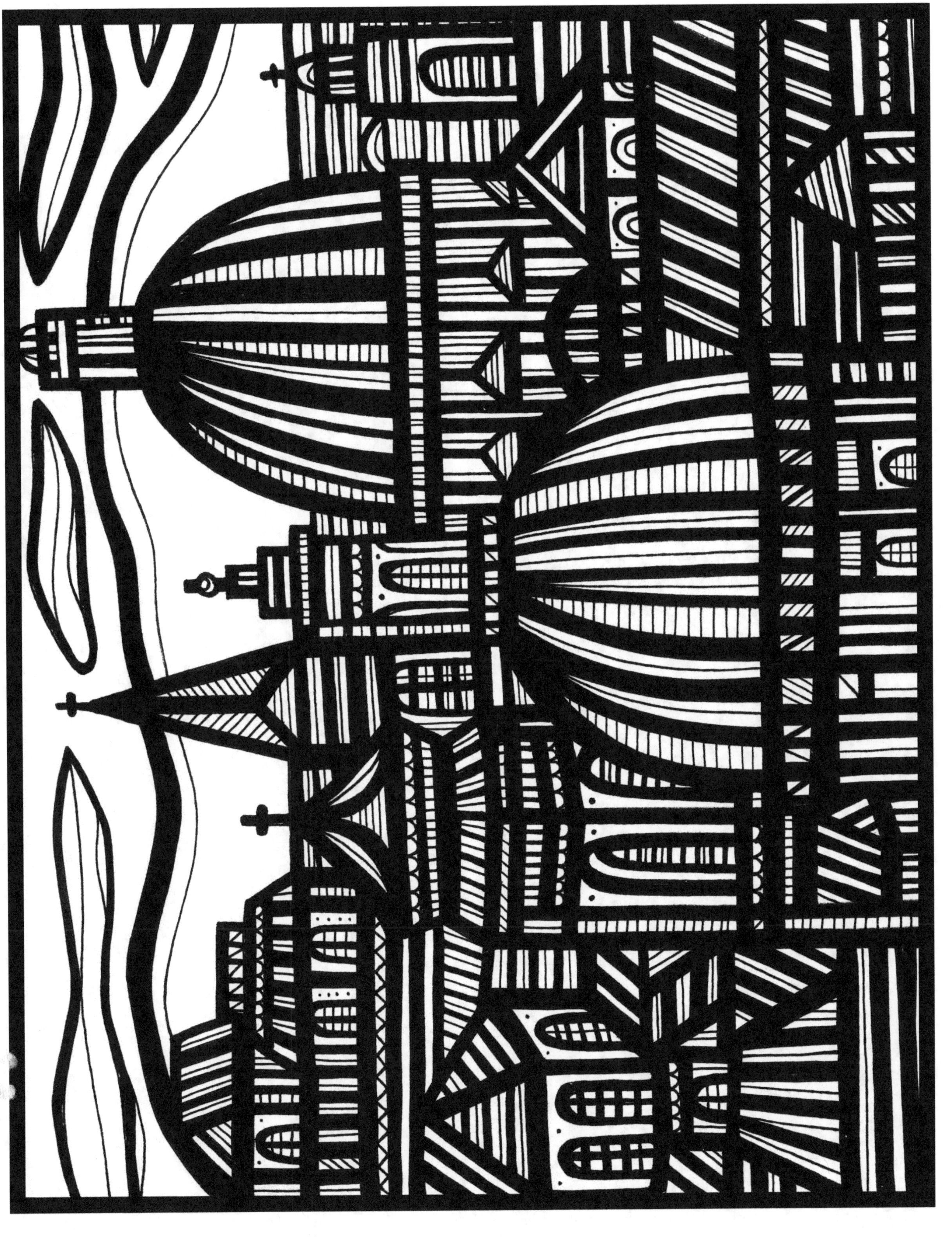

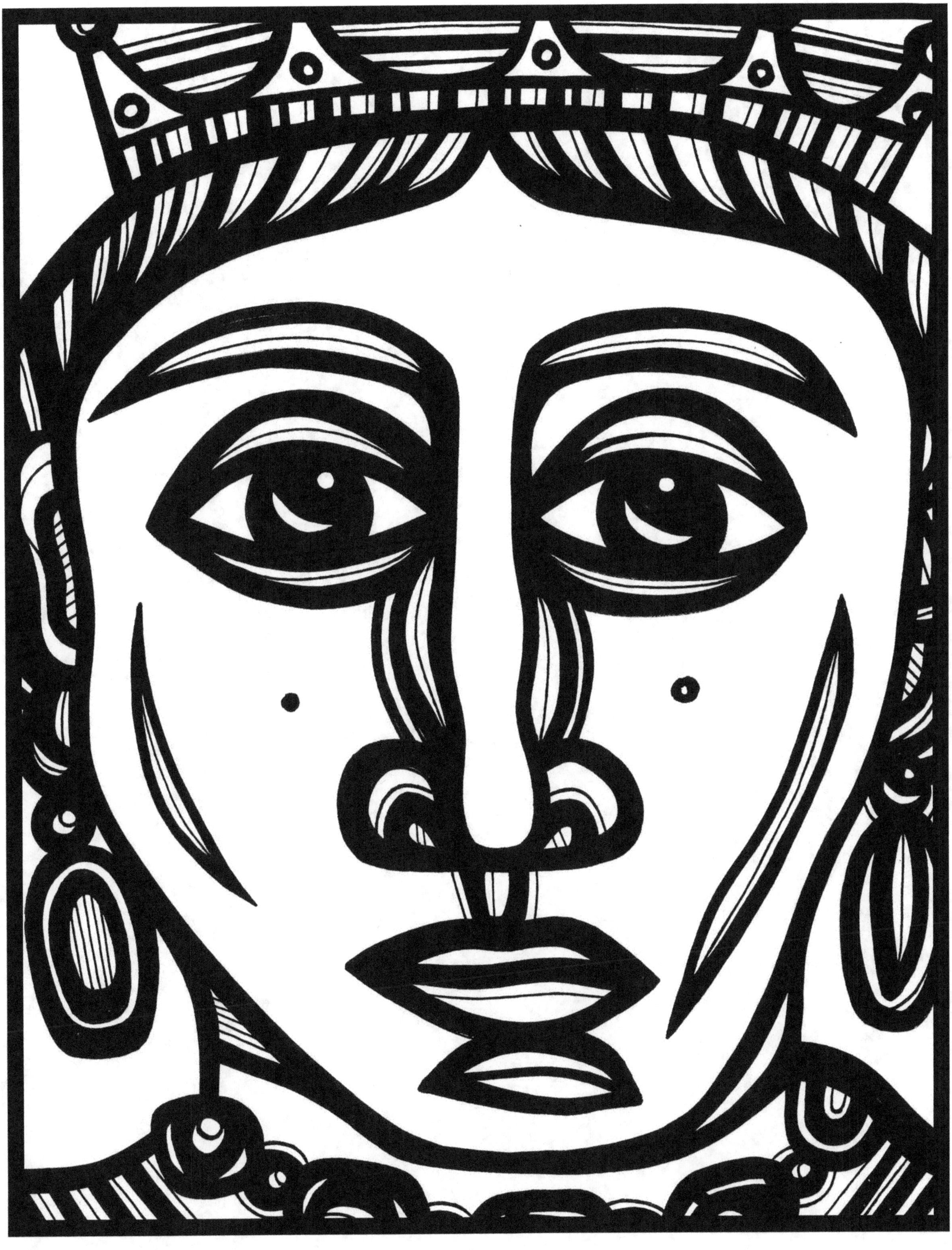

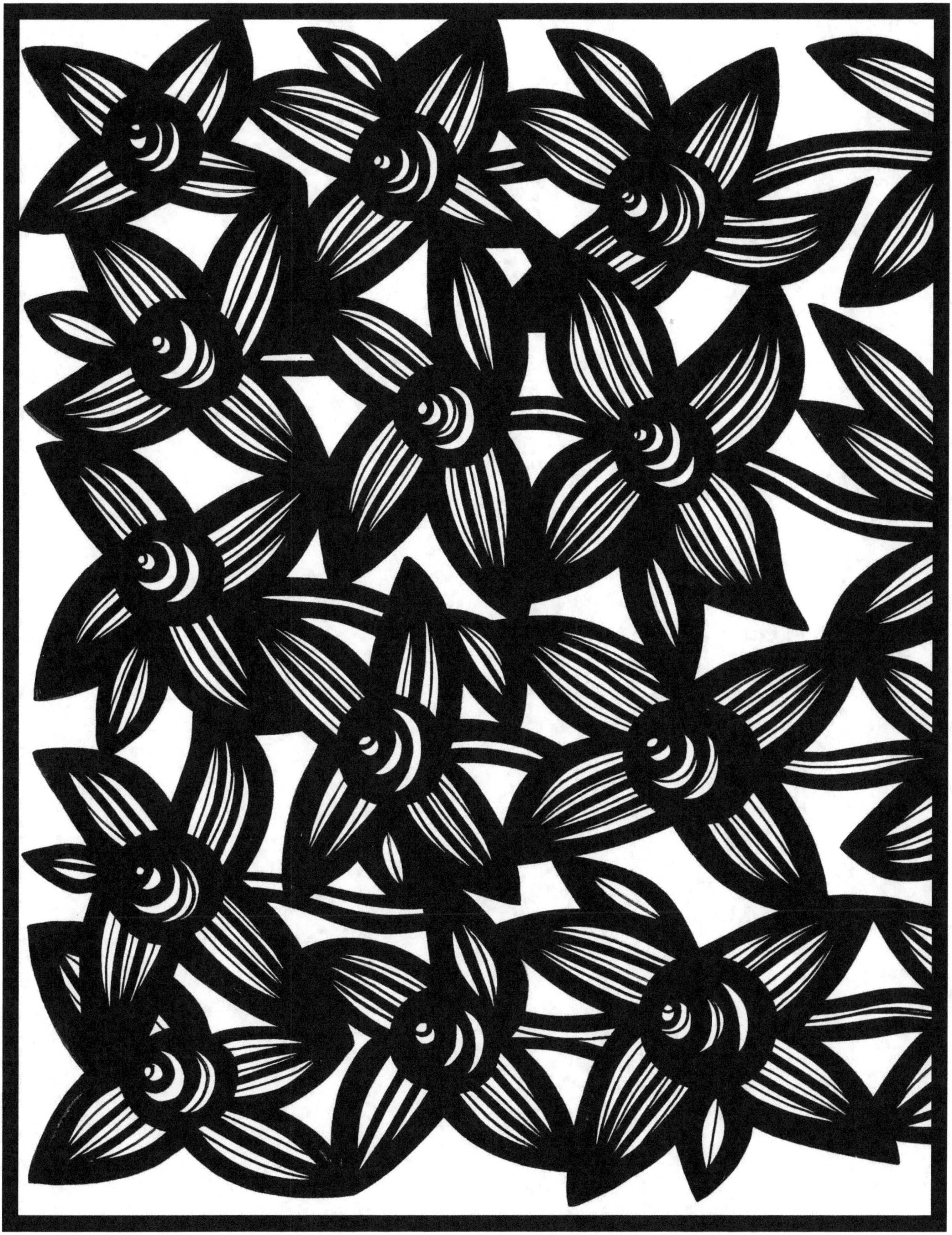

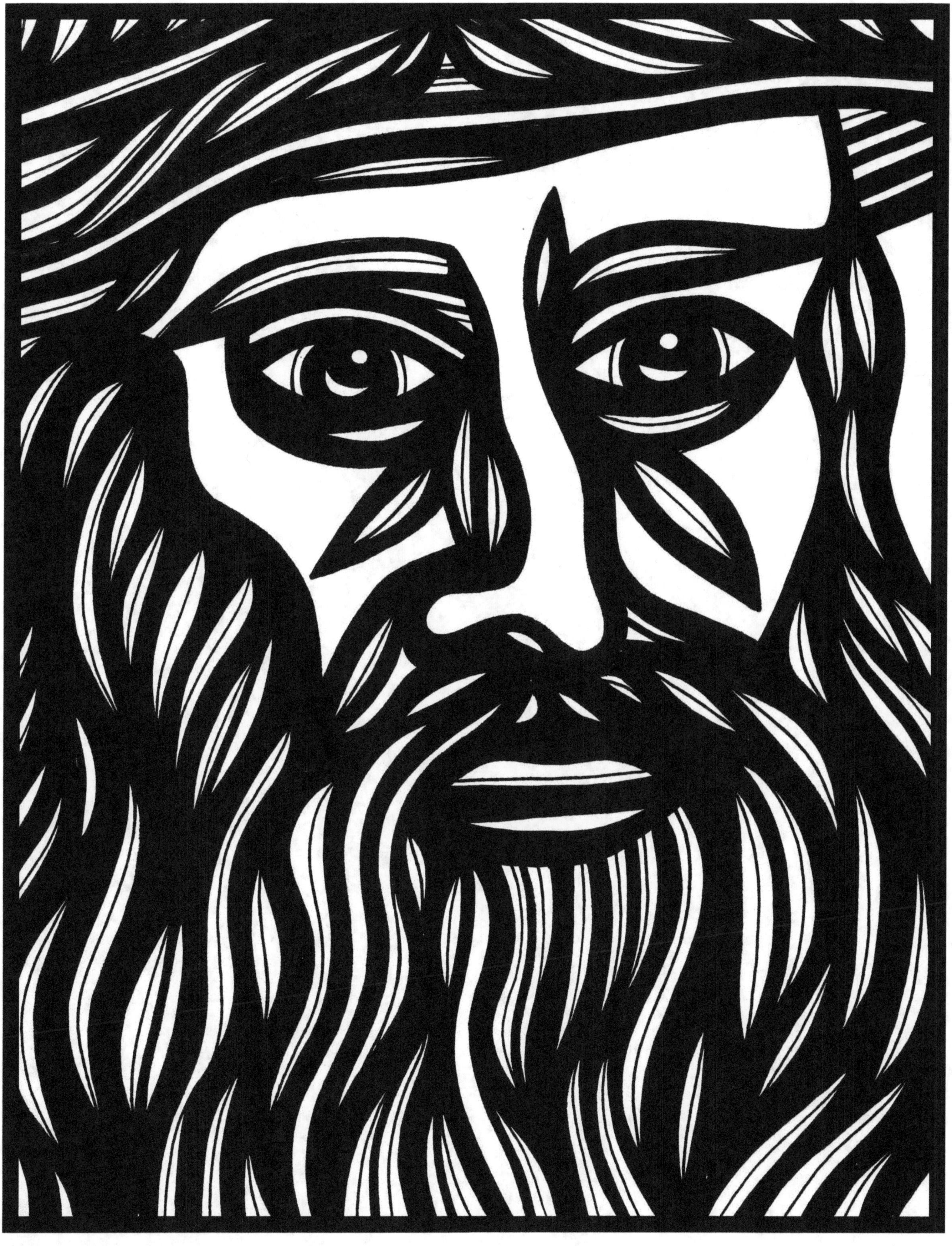

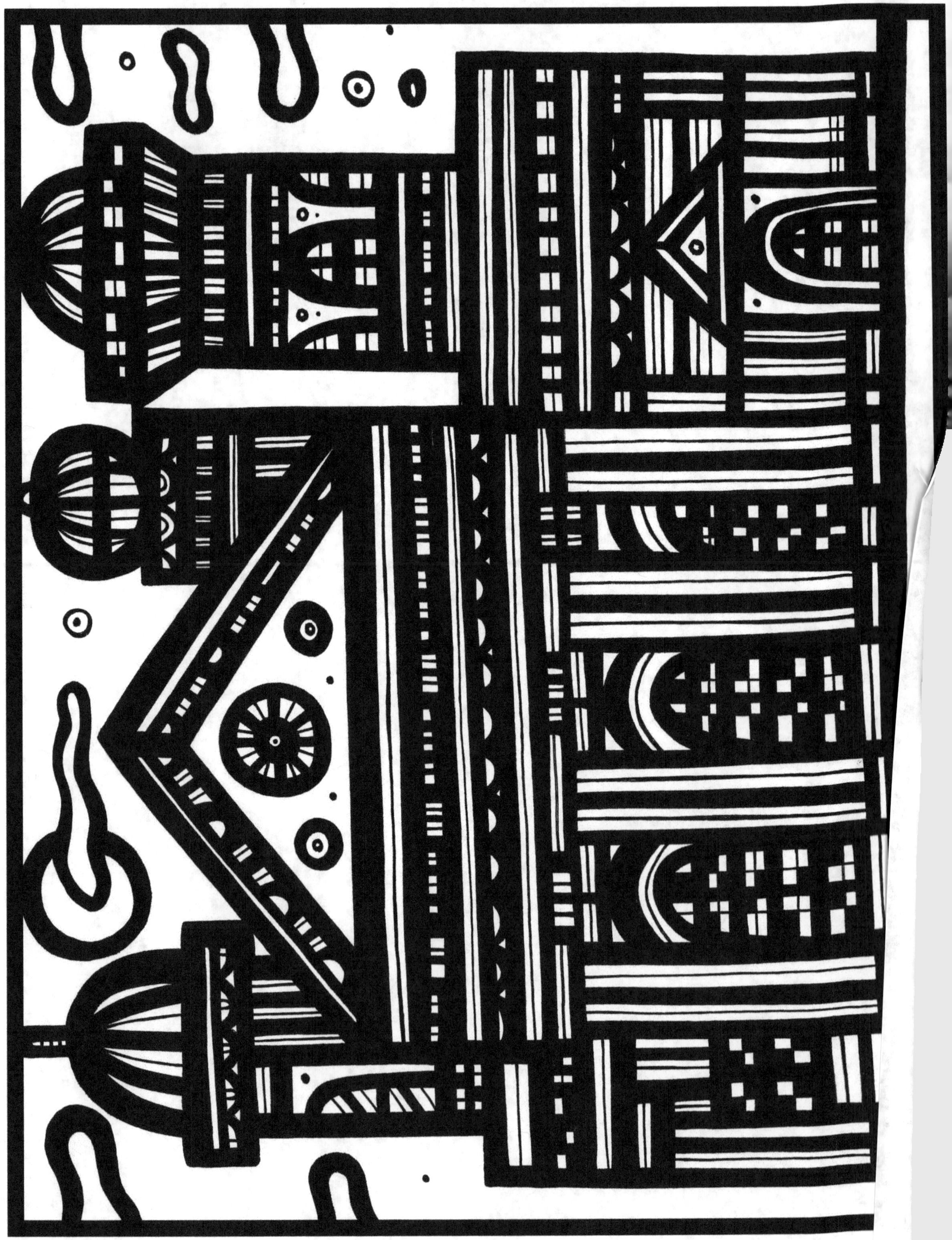

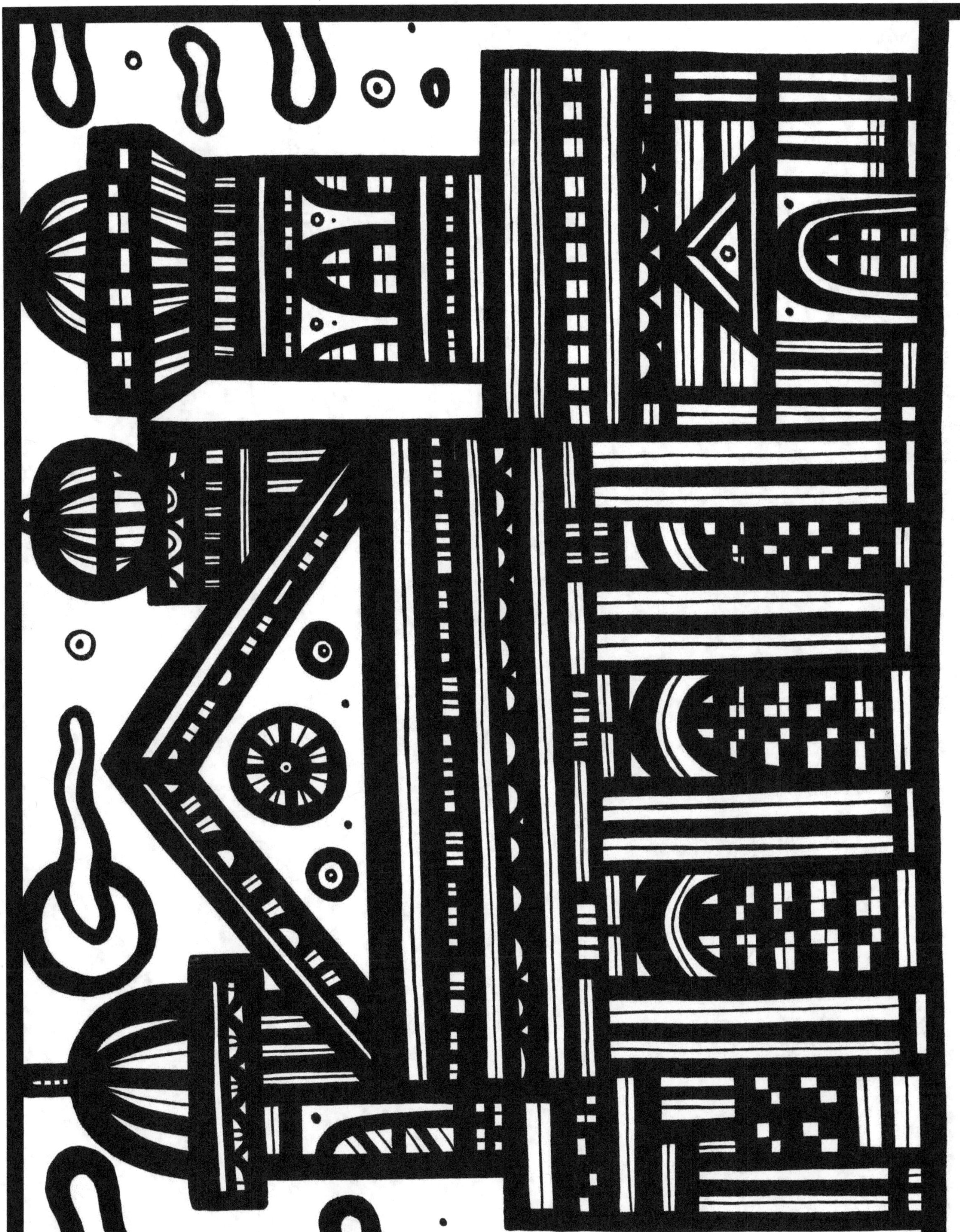

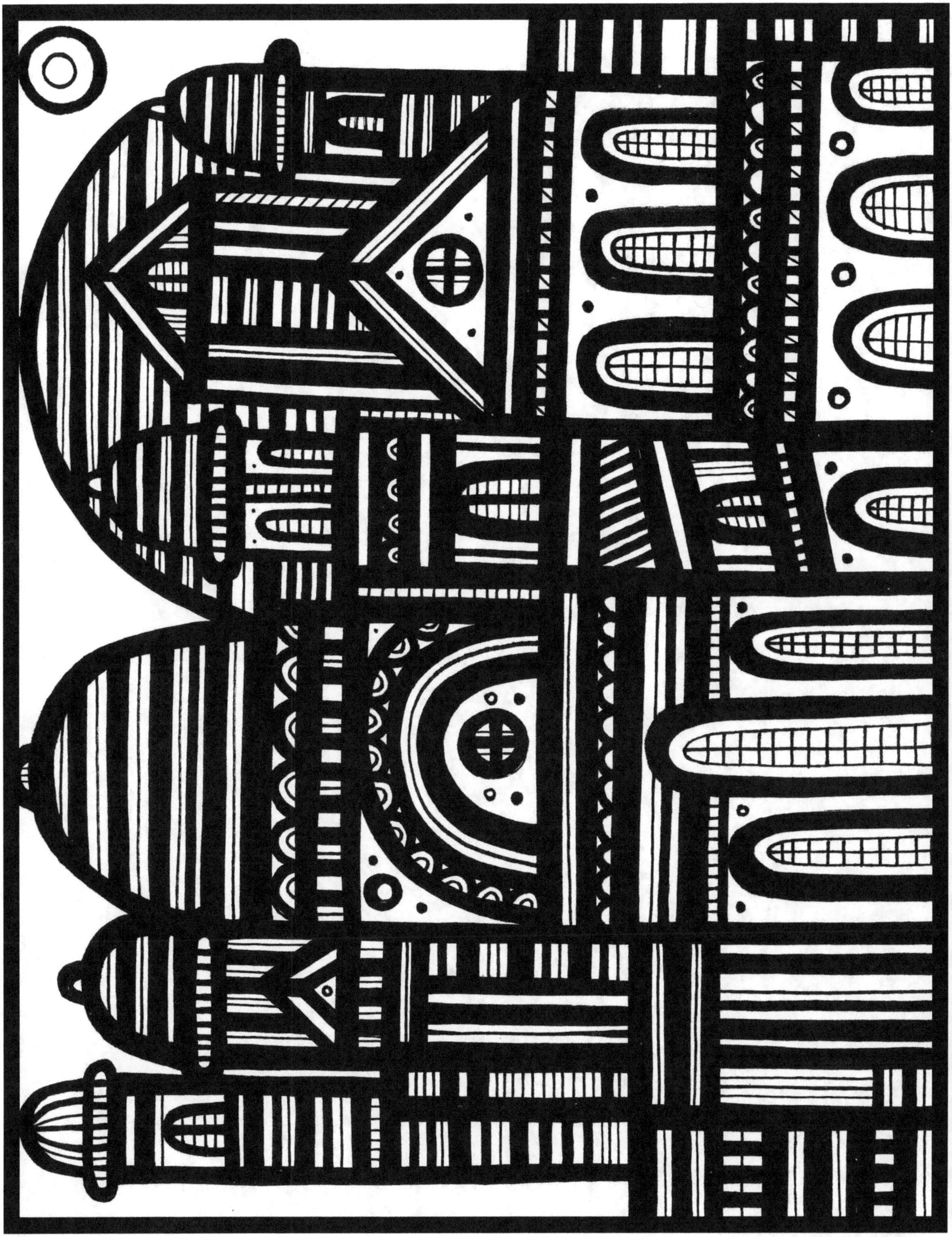

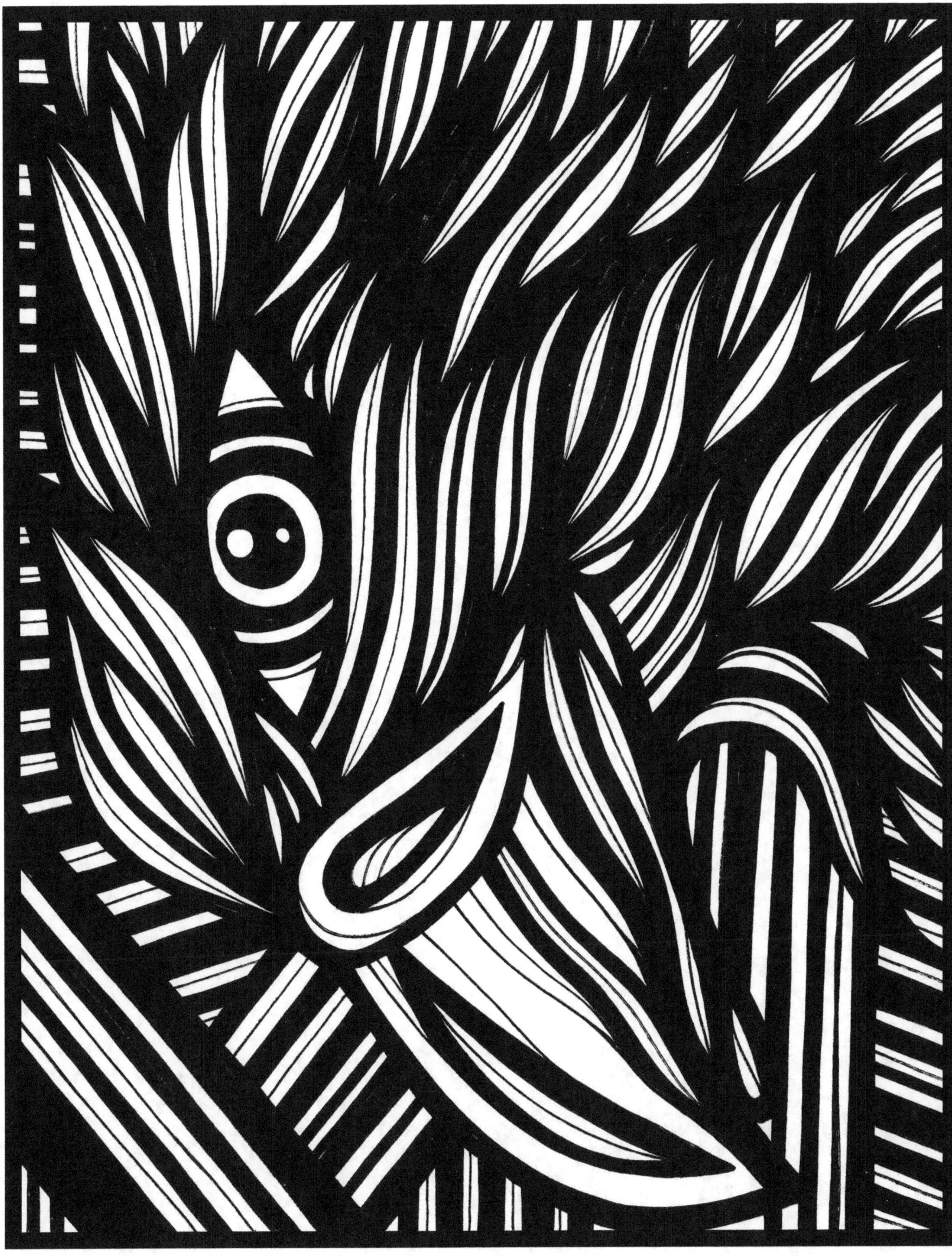

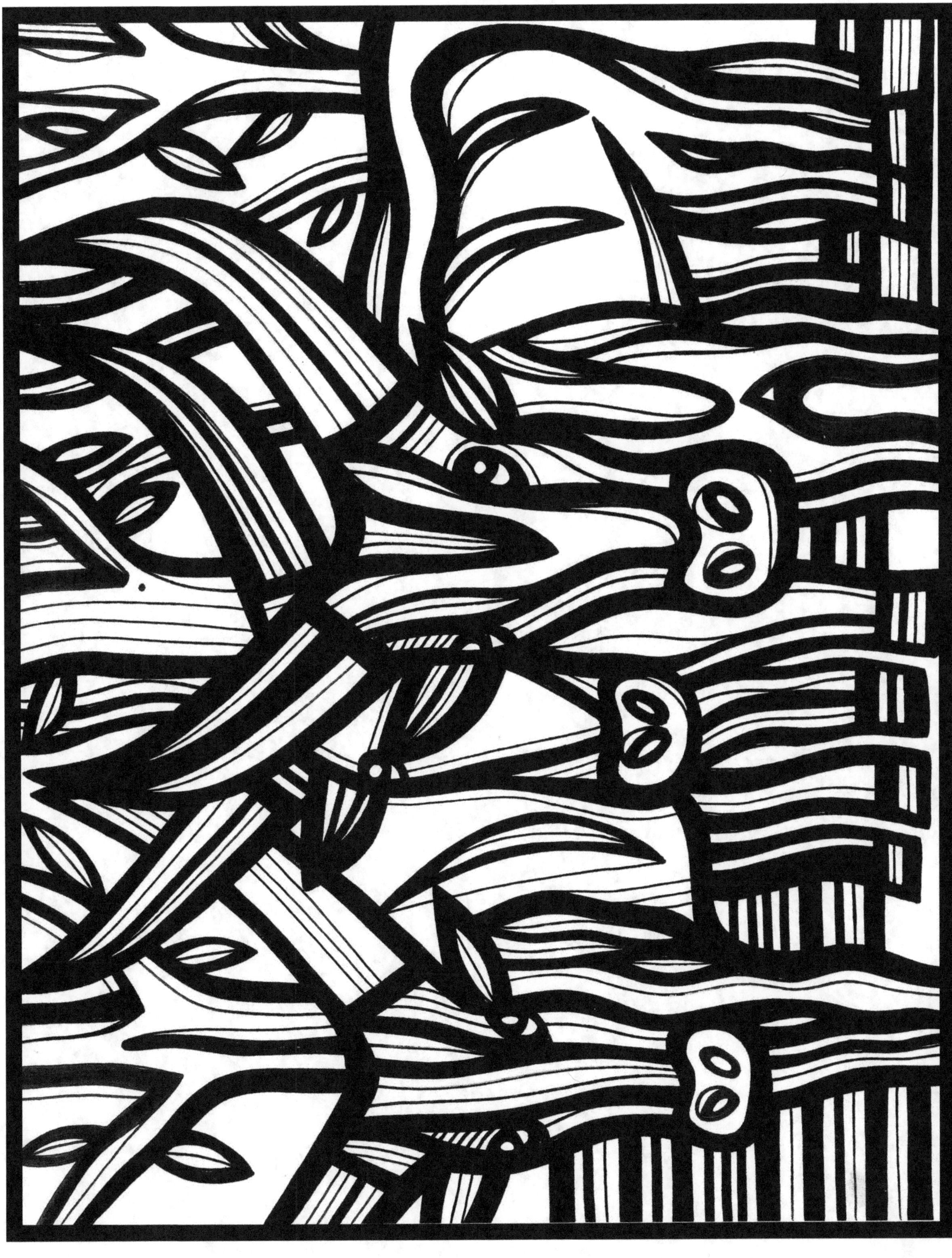

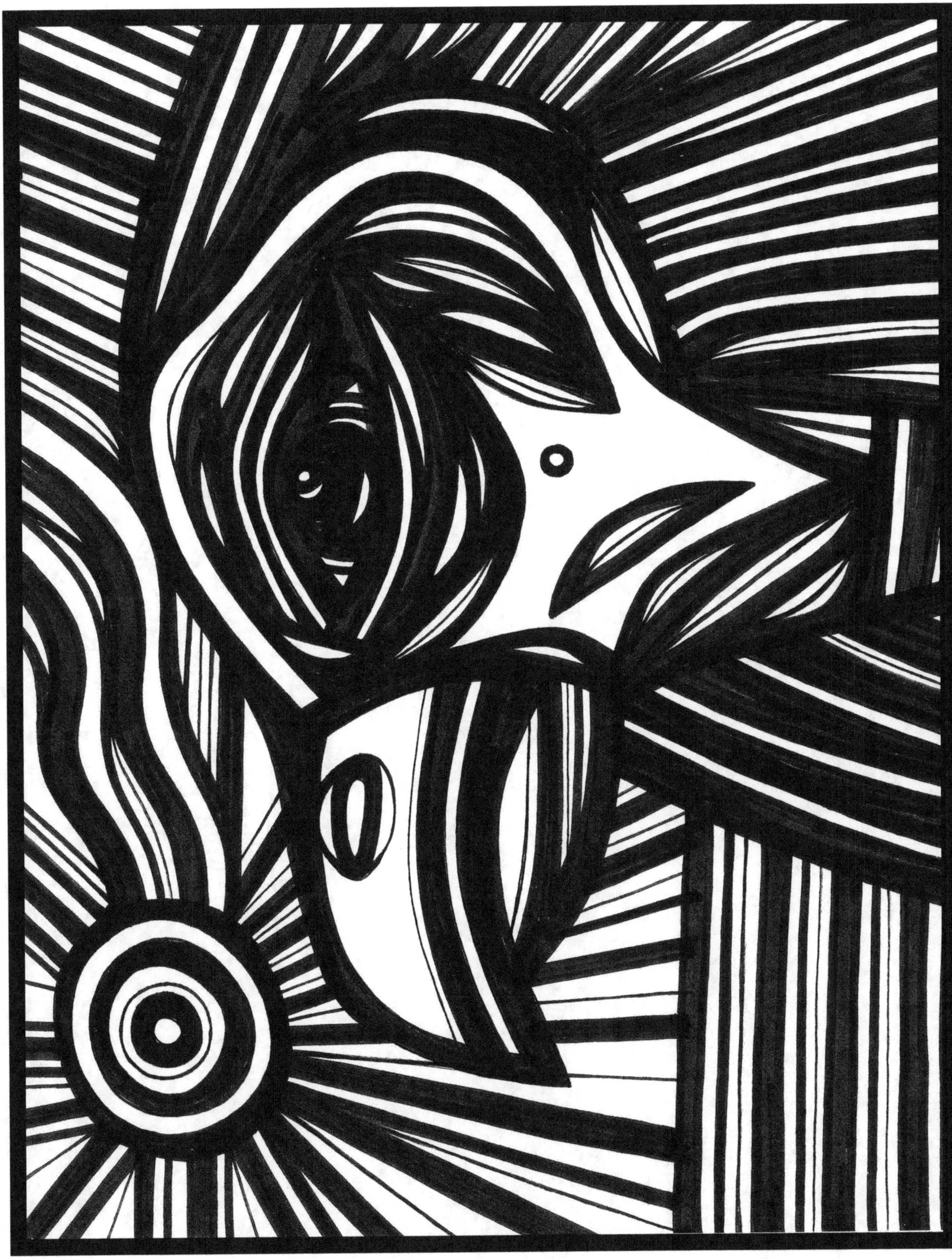

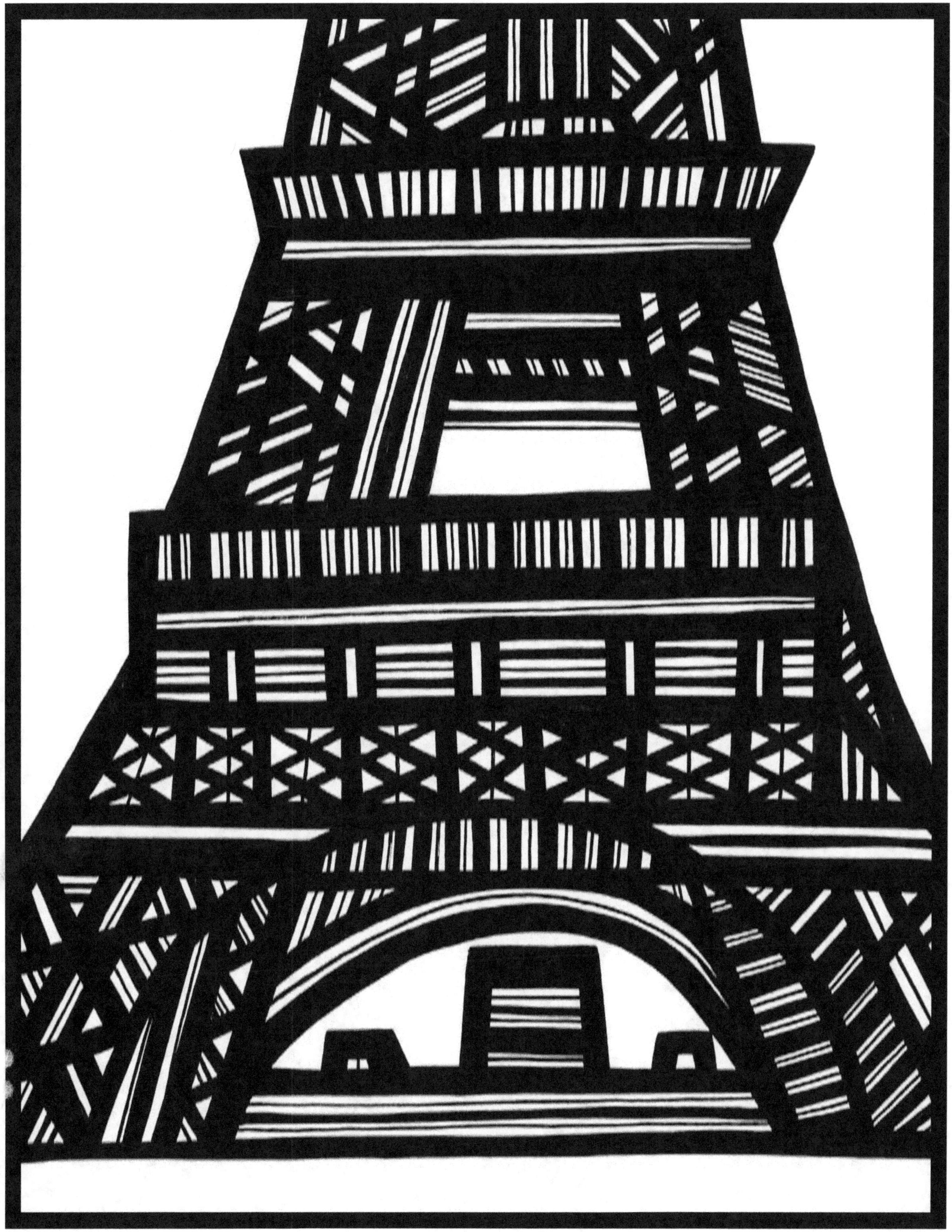

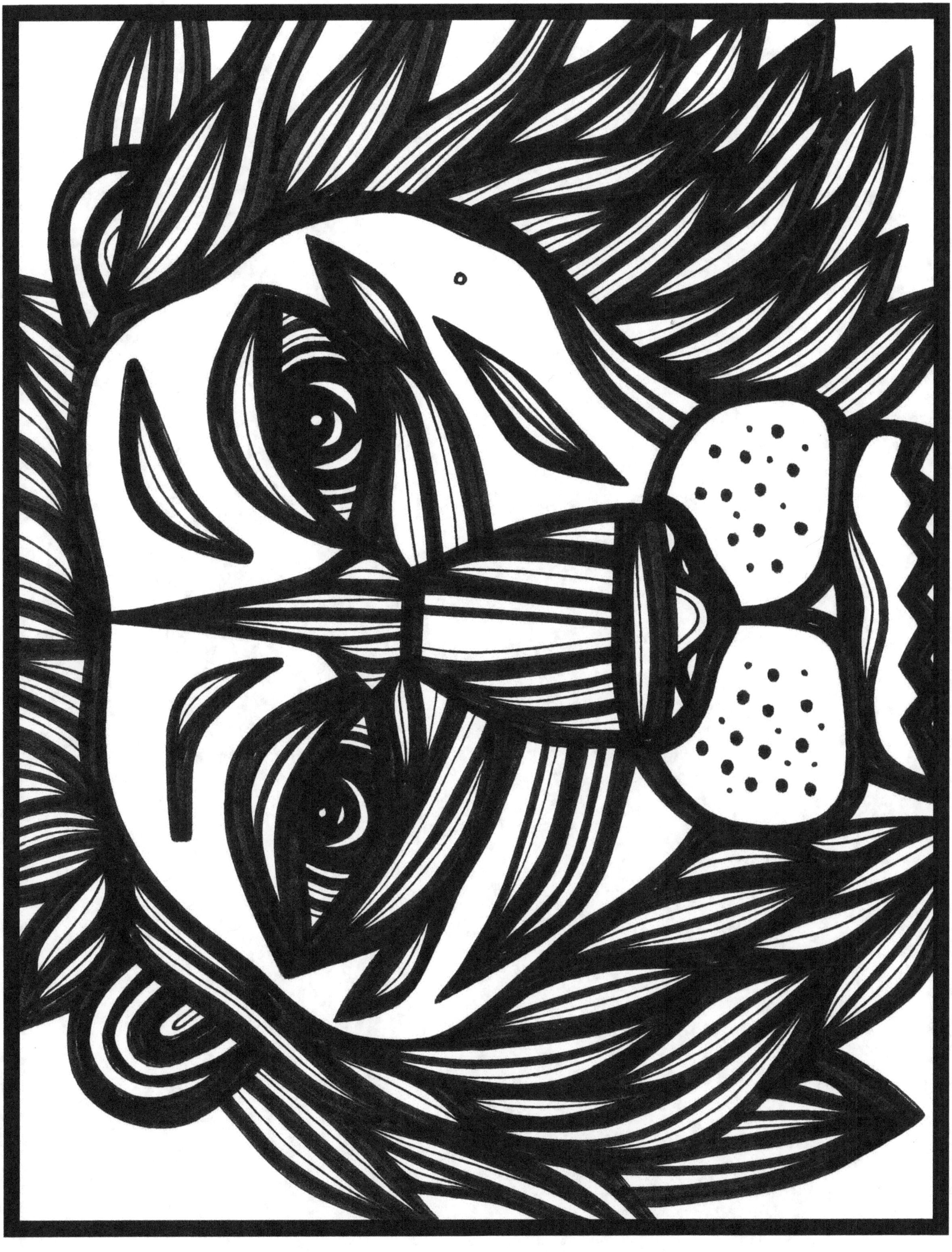

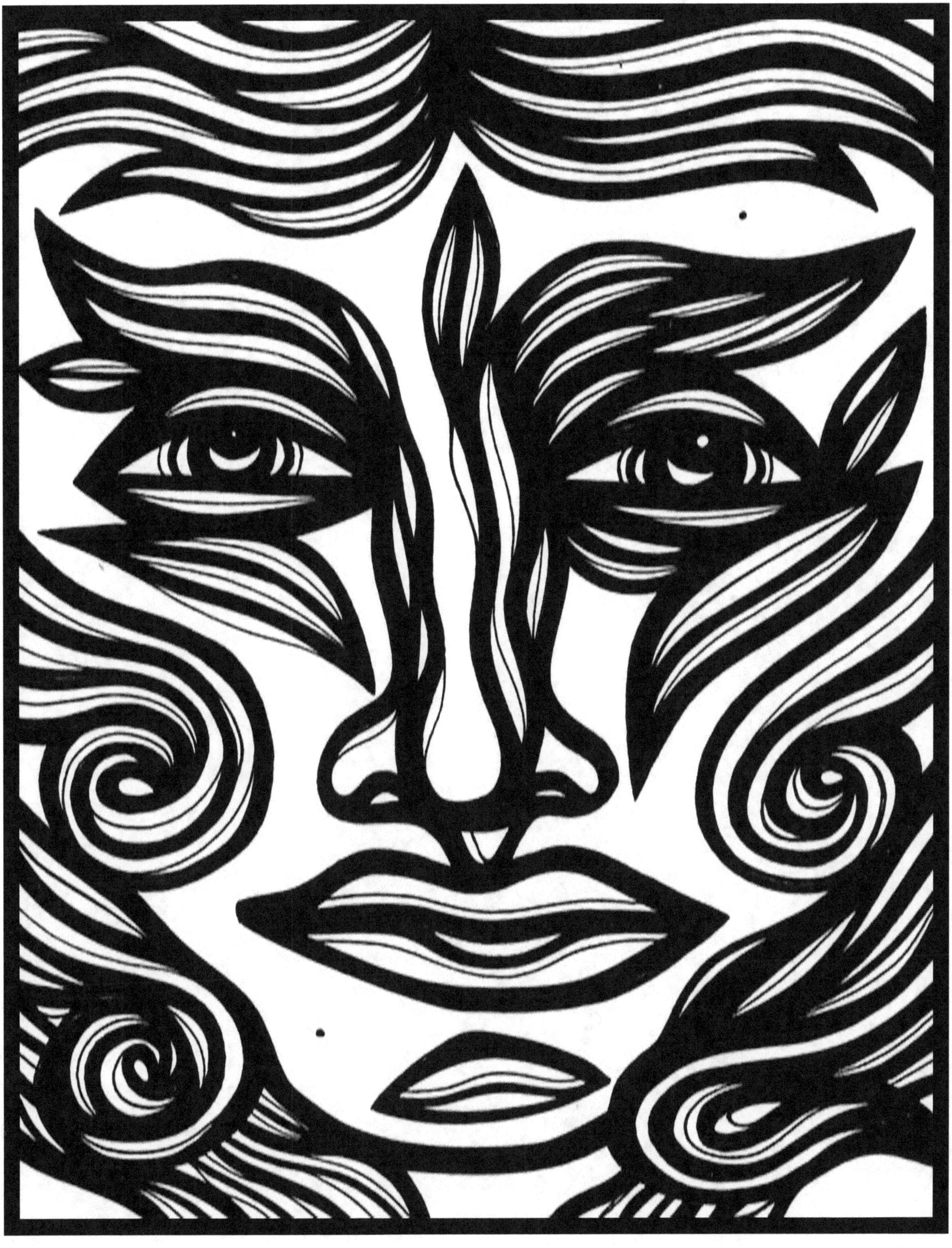

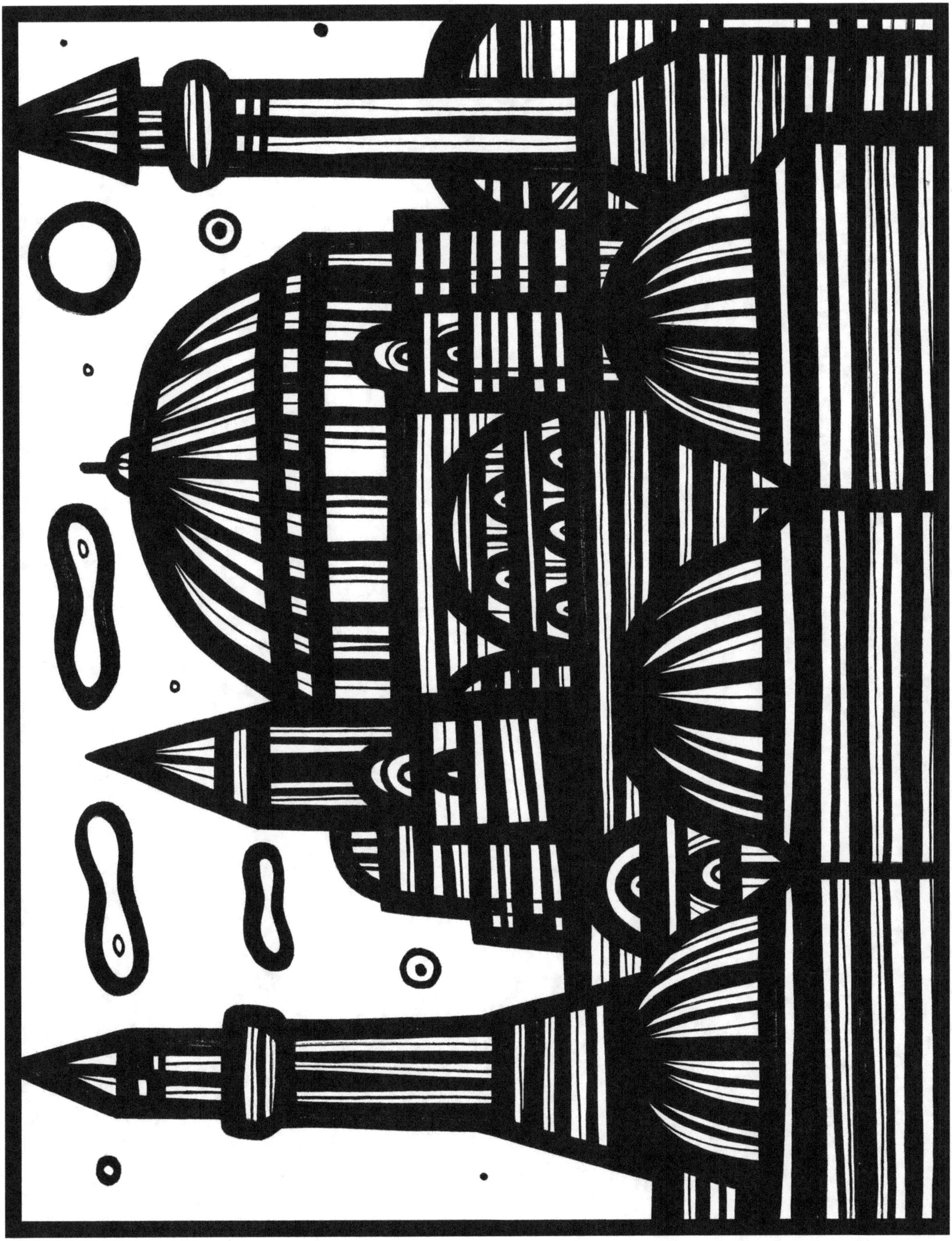

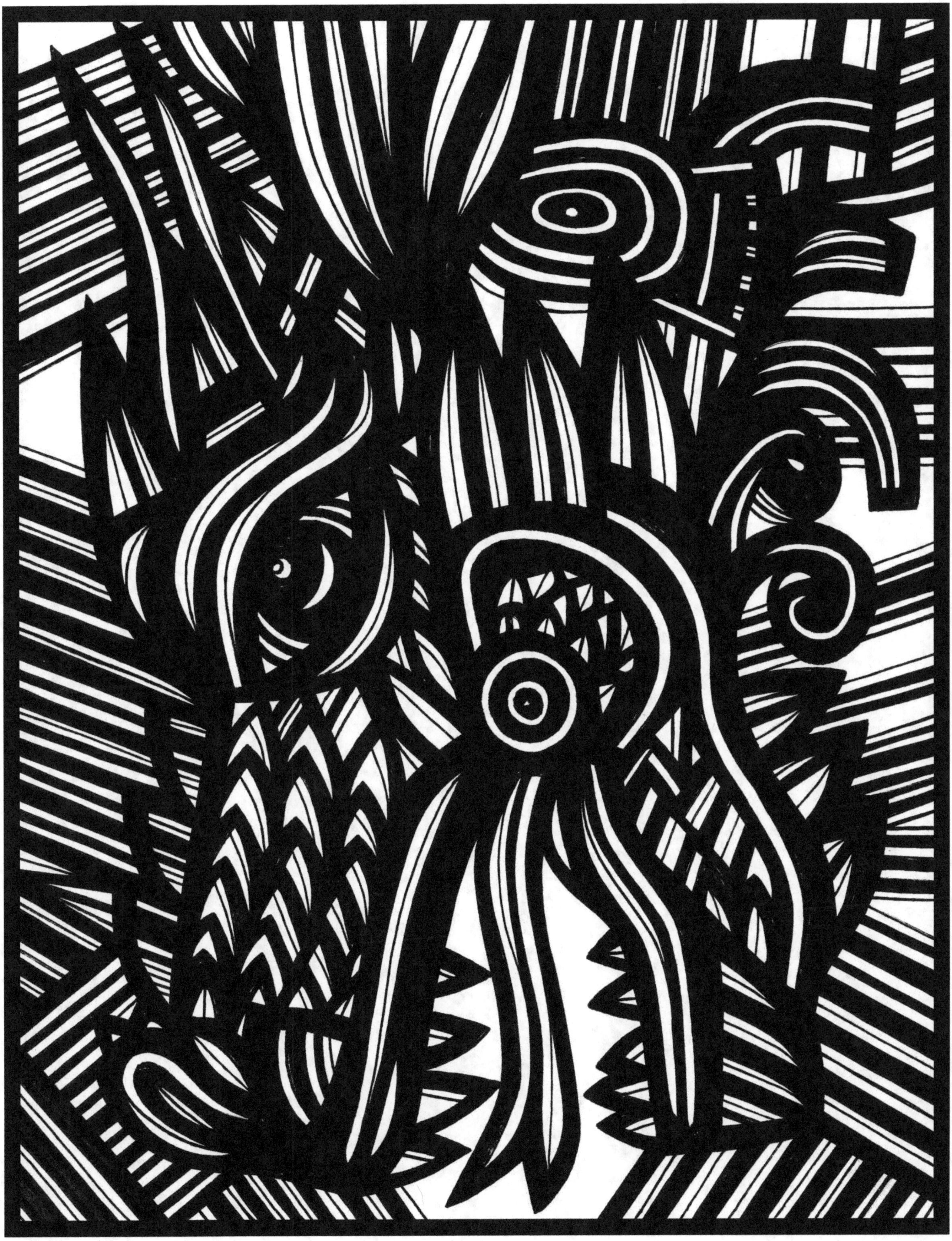

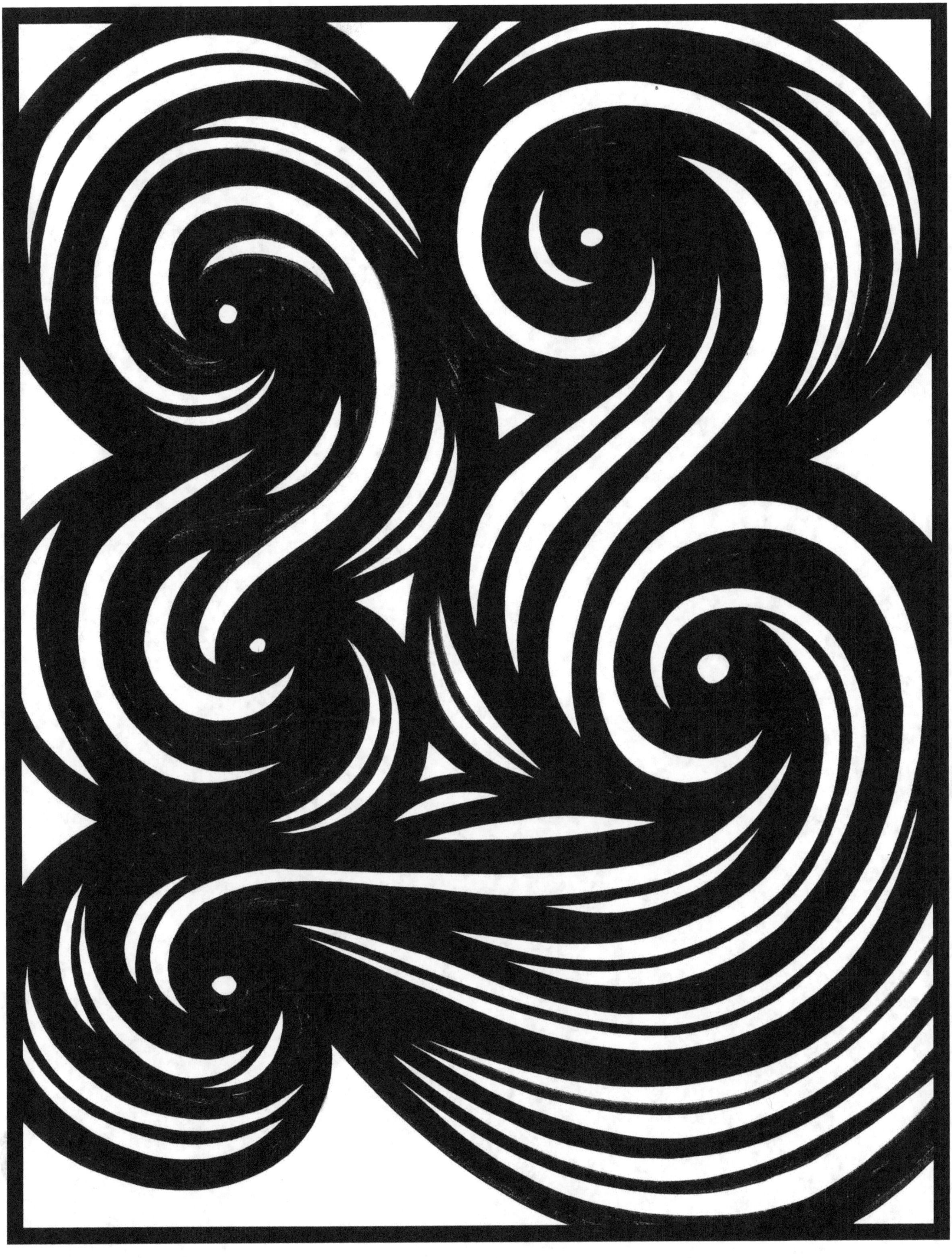

THE END, THANK YOU.

MORE BOOKS: 631ART.COM

www.ingramcontent.com/pod-product-compliance
Lightning Source LLC
Chambersburg PA
CBHW082014230526
45468CB00022B/2262
* 9 7 8 1 7 9 5 4 5 8 6 0 3 *